DO-IT-YOURSELF ENCYCLOPEDIA

A Practical Guide
to Home Improvement,
Repairs and Decorating
containing special material from
The Family Handyman
Do-It-Yourself Encyclopedia
and Family Circle.

Family Circle.

DO-IT-YOURSELF

ENCYCLOPEDIA

VOLUME **6** Ele-Fir

ROCKVILLE HOUSE PUBLISHERS, INC.

GARDEN CITY, NEW YORK 11530

Acknowledgments

The editors of this series would like to express their thanks and appreciation to the following for their assistance in preparing special sections within this encyclopedia, for their technical advice, and for photographs, art, charts and plans.

Allied Radio Corp. • Robert Malcomb Cook • George de Gennaro • Edison Electric Institute • Filon Corp. • Allen Green • Hedrich-Blessing • Home Insurance Co. • Jones & Jordal • Douglas Kirkland • Vincent Lisanti • Masonite Corp. • Monsanto Chemical Co. • Nicholson File Co. • George Nordhausen • Paul Paree • Propeller Fan Manufacturer's Assn. • Reynold's Aluminum • Robbins and Myers, Inc. • O. Philip Roedel • William Rosenthal • O. M. Scott & Sons • Ernest Silva • Stanley Tools • The Stanley Works • Uni-Built Div., Vega Industries, Inc.

Published by arrangement with
The Family Circle, Inc.,
a subsidiary of The New York Times Media Company, Inc.

Modern kitchen appliances and proper lighting for this household work center place heavy demands on the home's wiring circuits.

Electrical Wiring

The average handyman can do many electrical jobs around the house. BUT it is essential that he know exactly what he's doing and that he follow accepted electrical and safety rules. Before going any further, here is one rule to follow at all times: Do not touch any wire or fixture unless the current to that wire or fixture is OFF!

In this section on electrical wiring, you will find a basic explanation of wiring circuits, some terms commonly used, working hints when handling electrical wires and specific wiring problems and their solution. It is strongly recommended that you read through all the sections to obtain all the rules, working techniques and a basic understanding of what you are doing before you tackle an electrical job about the house.

Working with electricity is simple and a lot easier than doing masonry work. It is, however, more dangerous unless you know the rules. In some communities, only professional electricians are authorized to do any wiring in your home. In other areas, it is possible for the handyman to do the electrical work and have it inspected by local authorities.

When any wiring is to be done, whether it has to be inspected or not, the work must conform to standard wiring rules and regulations. Many of these rules are noted in the following sections. However, you should ask your local building authority for a copy of the local code, and also obtain the national wiring code from the Board of Fire Underwriters.

New Tools For Wiring

The tools you need for an electrical job depend upon the exact job you have in mind. Here, however, is a collection of tools which is useful

725

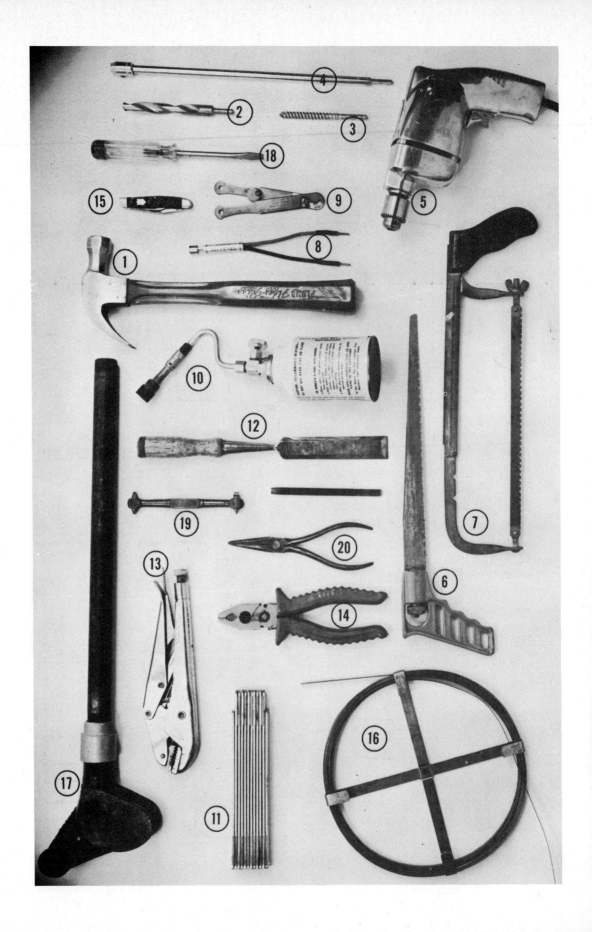

for interior and exterior wiring of all types: (See photo on next page).

1. Hammer—for driving nails, staples and fastening hangers.

2. Drill bit—one that will make a hole large enough for the electrical cable, BX or Romex, to pass through.

3. Masonry bit—needed if you have to make holes in concrete or brick walls.

4. Extension bit—a shaft extension to enable you to drill deep holes or to reach difficult-to-get-at places.

5. Drill—you can use a hand or electric drill or even a brace for boring holes.

6. Keyhole saw—for cutting holes and irregular shapes.

7. Hacksaw—for cutting BX cable, wire lath or wood lath and plaster.

8. Test light—this inexpensive unit is used to trace and test circuits, to check if the current is on or off in the cable as you work.

9. Wire stripper—this adjustable plier-like tool will quickly and easily strip the insulation off the wires you need for joining to switches, outlets, pilot lights or fixtures.

10. Blow torch—this liquefied petroleum torch is compact and convenient for an average handyman to use. It is needed to heat the wires when they are to be soldered.

11. Folding rule—for measuring distances, wire and openings.

12. Chisel—for notching studs, rafters, joists and lath to make an opening for the cable or conduit to pass through.

13. Lever-jaw wrench—can be used as a pliers, lock wrench and a pipe wrench while working.

14. Linesmen's pliers—this tool is used for cutting wires, gripping locknuts, etc. Note that the model shown in photograph has heavy rubber handles that form an insulation over the pliers as an added safety measure when working with wires.

15. Pocket knife—for cutting insulation and cleaning wires.

16. Fish tape—used to pull wire through a wall, floor or conduit.

17. Conduit bender—this 'hickey' will help you bend conduit in the approved manner. It is possible to bend the conduit without collapsing the walls of the tube or pipe.

18. Screwdriver — to tighten screws on connectors, switches and outlets and elsewhere when a screw has to be driven.

19. Offset screwdriver—to reach hard-to-get-at screws, especially inside of switch, outlet and junction boxes.

20. Long-nose pliers—helpful in bending ends of wire to fit under screw terminals.

New Materials for Wiring

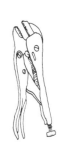

WIRE is your first requirement. Which type you use depends upon where the wire will be used and upon your local electrical code. You can use armored cable, commonly called BX cable, non-metallic sheathed cable, called Romex, rubber-covered cable or insulated wires through a conduit or pipe. It is best to use the same type of cable as is now used in your home, although this is not essential. However, adding BX cable to a home wired in Ro-

727

Three types of cable a handyman can use: BX or armored cable, Romex or non-metallic sheathed cable, or rubber-covered cable.

These switches NOT used on electrical lines are presented to show the details of single-pole double-pole, single-throw and double-throw operation. The one on the left is a DPDT—double-pole, double-throw switch. Note that the handle can be moved into the top or bottom position or left in the center. There are two wire terminals for each position, making it a double-pole, and there are two closed positions for the handle, making it a double-throw. The switch on the right is a DPST—double-pole, single-throw. The two wire terminals make it a double-pole, but there is only one closed position. Therefore, it is called a single throw.

728

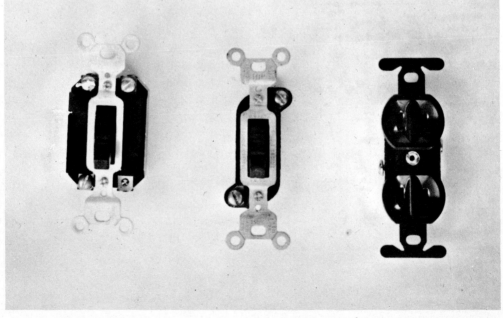

Standard electrical fixtures: three-way switch, SPST switch, double receptacle.

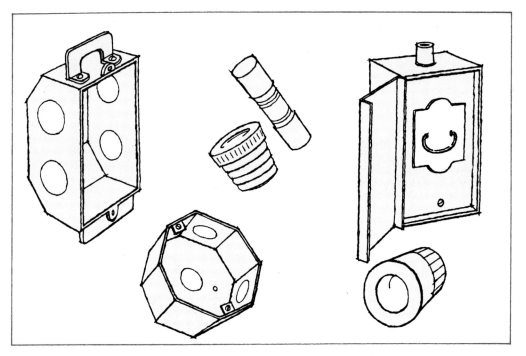

Some accessory items for electrical wiring jobs: outlet and junction boxes, solderless connector, fuse box, cartridge and glass fuses.

mex requires special grounding for the BX, and adding Romex to a home wired with BX requires the use of a grounding wire in the Romex so that all boxes are properly grounded.

The size of the wire is determined by the load it will carry. If the wire is to be used outdoors, it is necessary to use rubber-covered cable or insulated wires through pipe or conduit. Inside the home, you can use either Romex or BX, depending upon the local code requirements.

SWITCHES are used to make or break a line; that is, to close the circuit or open it. When the circuit is closed, the switch is in the 'on' position. When the circuit is open, the switch is in the 'off' position. Several different types of switches are used in the home:

1. The standard switch normally used is a SPST—single-pole, single-throw switch. That is, the switch is used only on one line—it is connected in series with the black or 'hot' wire. It can be opened or closed.

2. Another type of switch that can be used in special applications for the same purpose is a DPST—double-pole, single-throw switch. It is connected to both the white and black wires; it opens or closes both lines when the switch handle is moved.

3. When two switches are used to control a single light, a three-way switch is used. It is necessary to run a three-wire cable between the switches in this type of wiring. See

4. When three switches are used to control a single light, a four-way switch is necessary. This is a switch which has four terminal screws and is wired to two three-way switches as

729

shown in a wiring diagram later in this section.

OTHER MATERIALS—In addition to the wire, switches, outlets and pilot lights, you need outlet, switch or junction boxes, as well as connectors which secure the wire cable to the boxes.

1. A switch box, usually rectangular in shape, can be used to house a switch or even an outlet.

2. A junction box, usually octagonal in shape, is used for the joining of wires or for attaching a light fixture.

3. An outlet box, usually a shallow rectangular shaped unit, is used to house an outlet.

You also need solderless connectors or solder and tape for joining the wires, and straps or staples to anchor the cable to the wall and joists as it is installed.

Wiring Symbols

The following electrical symbols are used in house plans and blueprints. They will help you read the plans more intelligently and also enable the handyman to figure out special wiring circuits.

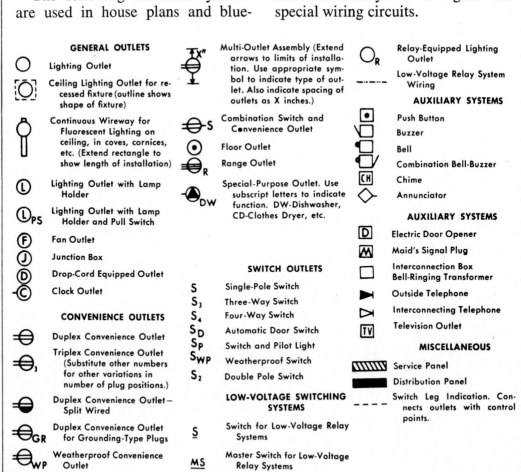

GENERAL OUTLETS

- Lighting Outlet
- Ceiling Lighting Outlet for recessed fixture (outline shows shape of fixture)
- Continuous Wireway for Fluorescent Lighting on ceiling, in coves, cornices, etc. (Extend rectangle to show length of installation)
- Lighting Outlet with Lamp Holder
- Lighting Outlet with Lamp Holder and Pull Switch
- Fan Outlet
- Junction Box
- Drop-Cord Equipped Outlet
- Clock Outlet

CONVENIENCE OUTLETS

- Duplex Convenience Outlet
- Triplex Convenience Outlet (Substitute other numbers for other variations in number of plug positions.)
- Duplex Convenience Outlet — Split Wired
- Duplex Convenience Outlet for Grounding-Type Plugs
- Weatherproof Convenience Outlet

Multi-Outlet Assembly (Extend arrows to limits of installation. Use appropriate symbol to indicate type of outlet. Also indicate spacing of outlets as X inches.)

Combination Switch and Convenience Outlet

Floor Outlet

Range Outlet

Special-Purpose Outlet. Use subscript letters to indicate function. DW-Dishwasher, CD-Clothes Dryer, etc.

SWITCH OUTLETS

S	Single-Pole Switch
S_3	Three-Way Switch
S_4	Four-Way Switch
S_D	Automatic Door Switch
S_P	Switch and Pilot Light
S_{WP}	Weatherproof Switch
S_2	Double Pole Switch

LOW-VOLTAGE SWITCHING SYSTEMS

| $\underline{S}$ | Switch for Low-Voltage Relay Systems |
| $\underline{MS}$ | Master Switch for Low-Voltage Relay Systems |

Relay-Equipped Lighting Outlet

Low-Voltage Relay System Wiring

AUXILIARY SYSTEMS

- Push Button
- Buzzer
- Bell
- Combination Bell-Buzzer
- Chime
- Annunciator

AUXILIARY SYSTEMS

- Electric Door Opener
- Maid's Signal Plug
- Interconnection Box Bell-Ringing Transformer
- Outside Telephone
- Interconnecting Telephone
- Television Outlet

MISCELLANEOUS

- Service Panel
- Distribution Panel
- Switch Leg Indication. Connects outlets with control points.

730

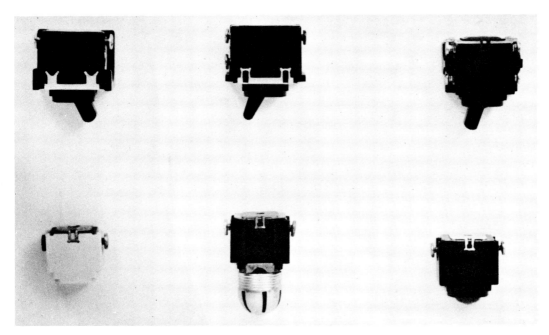

These are Despard electric fixtures; several can be mounted within a special plate in a single box. From upper left across: SPST, 3-way switch, 4-way switch; bottom row across: outlet, pilot light, neon pilot light.

Electrical Terms You Should Know

While electrical engineering is a complex subject reserved for the professionals, it is essential that the handyman be familiar with certain basic terms before he starts any electrical project. As you read through this list, you'll be amazed at all the terms with which you are already familiar even though you might have done only a few simple wiring jobs. However, for the sake of clarity and safety in following the detailed instructions given later in this section, here are several of the more important terms together with their meaning:

AC—Alternating current: the type of power used in most home wiring systems; usually 60 cycles, but 25- and 50-cycle systems are used in a few localities.

AMPERE—This is a unit of measure of the rate of flow of electricity, something like the gallons per minute in a water system.

BUSHING—An insulator which fits around the wires at the end of a BX cable to prevent the cut metal from fraying the insulation covering the wires.

CIRCUIT—The complete flow of electricity is traced through what is technically called a circuit; it is the flow of current through a wire for the source of supply to one or more outlets and then back to the source of supply through another wire.

CIRCUIT-BREAKER—It performs the same function as a fuse in opening or breaking the circuit when there is an overload of current, but needs only to be reset.

CONDUCTORS—The trade name for electric wires.

CONDUIT—This is metal tubing

resembling pipe through which wires are run; it is used frequently when running wires underground or in areas where exposed wires are in danger of being frayed, broken or cut.

BX—Common trade term used for armored cable.

CONNECTOR—Also called a BX connector, this fitting is used to secure the conductors to an outlet, junction or switch box.

DC—Direct current: the type of power still used in some areas for home wiring; also the current flow from batteries where one wire is always 'positive' or 'negative' or ground.

FUSE—A safety device which breaks the flow of current or electricity whenever a circuit is overloaded.

GROUNDING—The connection of the electrical system to the earth, a precaution necessary to prevent damage from lightning and to minimize the danger from shocks.

H.P.—Horsepower; a unit of measure of work; one H.P. equals 746 watts.

HOT WIRES—The power-carrying wires, usually black or red, as distinguished from the neutral wires, usually white.

INSULATION — A protective sheathing used over wires to prevent the escape of electricity.

JUNCTION BOX—A metal box, either square or octagonal, in which wires from different circuits are joined.

OUTLET—A device or fixture that permits tapping off electricity at convenient locations for lights or appliances.

OUTLET BOX—A unit in which

732

an outlet or to which a fixture such as a ceiling light is secured and joined to the wiring system.

OVERLOAD—Term used to describe an electrical condition in which too much current is flowing through the line for the fuse controlling that particular line.

POLARIZING — Identification of wires by color throughout the entire system to help assure that hot wires will be connected only to hot wires and that neutral wires run in a continuous uninterrupted connection back to the ground terminal.

RECEPTACLE—Similar to outlet; a unit to which electric cords can be plugged in conveniently.

ROMEX—Term used for non-metallic sheathed cable.

SERVICE ENTRANCE SWITCH —Technical name for a fuse box; it is the main panel through which electricity is brought into the building and then distributed to various branch circuits. It contains the main disconnect switch for the entire wiring system as well as fuses or circuit-breakers for the individual lines.

SHORT CIRCUIT—Popularly called a 'short,' it is an improper connection between hot wires or between a hot wire and a neutral wire.

SWITCH—A device for breaking the flow of current.

SWITCH BOX—A metal unit, usually a rectangle but can be square, in which a switch or switches are connected to the circuit.

THREE-WAY SWITCH—A type of switch which is used in pairs to control the same light from two different points.

UNDERWRITERS' LABORATORIES—A nationally accepted organization which tests all types of wiring materials and devices to make certain that they meet minimum standards for safety and quality. If the item meets their approval, it usually carries a UL seal or tag. Don't take chances with inferior materials—look for the UL seal or tag when you buy.

VOLT—This is a unit used in measuring electrical pressure, like pounds in a water system.

VOLTAGE DROP—This term is used to indicate the loss of voltage which occurs when wires are overloaded or when the current has to travel a great distance through a wire.

WATT—This unit shows the current drain taking into account both voltage and amperage. For example, 1 watt is equal to 1 ampere at 1 volt, or 75 watts on a bulb indicates that the bulb consumes about .64 (slightly more than 6/10ths) of an ampere at 115 volts.

WATT HOUR—One watt used for one hour equals 1 watt hour; 1,000 watt hours equals 1 kilowatt hour (Kwh), which is the unit by which electricity is metered.

Adequate Wiring
For Your Home

Adequate wiring in your home depends upon (a) the load which the service entrance lines will carry to your home, and (b) the number of branch circuits to carry full power to the appliances and lighting fixtures. Today's home has many more appliances than homes of 10 or 20 years ago. Now there are washing machines, clothes dryers, freezers, air conditioners, TV sets—appliances commonly found in the home today which were not present years back.

The addition of more appliances puts a greater strain on the electrical wires. You just cannot keep adding appliances in a home without providing for more current to enter a home. Just as an analogy—if you were to add four or five bathtubs to your home today without changing the main water pipe, you would not expect the tubs to be filled at the same rate as the single tub is today. The same is true of electricity. As you add appliances, it is necessary to increase the load-carrying capacity of the service wires.

Check with your local public utilities to determine what size wires are used in your service connection box and what load they are meant to carry. A #6 wire should be used for the service entrance, or a #4; if there is any doubt, it's better to use a #4, for you will always have additional current capacity available.

Here are some standard arrangements for service entrance hook-ups:

1. For minimum service you should have 3-wire #6 service conductors—usually 115-230 volts with a 60-ampere switch or fuse. This will provide for a range circuit, three 15-ampere branch circuits and one 20-ampere branch circuit.

2. For maximum service, you should have 3-wire #4 service conductors—115-230 volts with a 100-ampere switch or fuse. This is the size required for a seven-circuit installation in a home.

733

Branch Circuits

The service conductors are divided into branches so that if an overload or short occurs in one circuit, only the fuse of that circuit will be affected. The current in the rest of the lines will continue while the current in only the one line will stop.

You must have at least one 20-ampere appliance circuit for your kitchen and laundry area. This circuit should be independent of the lights in those rooms. It is best to have one separate circuit for the kitchen and another for the laundry.

A separate 15-ampere lighting circuit is recommended for every 500 square feet of floor space in your home. These circuits can be used to power the room lights, radios, fans and other smaller appliances.

Heavier appliances require additional circuits. It is best to check the load on each circuit before introducing another item. A room space heater, for example, draws about 10 amperes. You can readily see what would happen if it were connected in a circuit which is already drawing about 15 amperes or even 10 amperes. The fuse would blow because too much current is passing through the line. See the accompanying tables showing the average wattage of appliances in the home.

The Wattage Requirements of Portable Appliances		
Appliances	Number	Average Wattages
1. Bed Covering	1 to 2	185
2. Bottle Warmer	1	400
3. Broiler	1	1325
4. Clock	3 to 5	2
5. Coffee Maker (Automatic)	1 to 2	830
6. Cooker (Egg)	1	520
7. Fan (Desk)	1 to 3	70
8. Floor Polisher	1	240
9. Fruit Extractor	1	80
10. Germicidal Lamp	1 to 3	20
11. Grill	1	770
12. Hair Dryer	1	235
13. Heater (Radiant)	1 to 2	1095
14. Heating Pad	1 to 2	55
15. Heat Lamp (Infra-red)	1 to 3	250
16. Hot Plate	1	1140
17. Iron (Hand)	1 to 2	1000
18. Mixer (Food)	2 to 6	120
19. Percolator	1 to 2	490
20. Radio	2 to 6	90
21. Radio Phonograph	1 to 2	100
22. Razor (Electric)	1 to 2	15
23. Roaster	1	1300
24. Sewing Machine	1	75
25. Sun Lamp	1 to 3	390
26. Television	1 to 2	280
27. Toaster	1 to 2	990
28. Vacuum Cleaner	1 to 2	315
29. Vibrator	1	45
30. Waffle Baker	1	855

The Wattage Requirements of Major Appliances in the Home	
Fixed Appliances	**Average Wattage**
KITCHEN	
1. Refrigerator	205
2. Range	10800
3. Fan	85
4. Dishwasher	1155
5. Food Waste Disposer	330
LAUNDRY	
6. Water Heater	2500
7. Automatic Washer	1000
8. Clothes Dryer	4350
9. Ironer	1500
UTILITY ROOM	
10. Furnace Fan	225
11. Oil Burner	245
12. Stoker	250
13. Heat Pump	3 & 5 HP
14. Electronic Air Cleaner	60
15. Air Conditioner (Central)	(2 to 5 HP)
16. Water Pump	265
17. Dehumidifier	210
18. Home Freezer	255
MISCELLANEOUS	
19. Attic Fan	370
20. Room Air Conditioner	800
21. Bathroom Heater	1095

Source: Edison Electric Institute

When the Fuse Blows

When a fuse blows or burns out, it is a sign that you may have an overload or a short circuit. It's easy to see if a plug-type fuse is burned out, but cartridge fuses do not change in appearance.

It is a good idea to have a list of the switches, outlets and lights that each fuse controls pasted on the inside of the cover of the fuse box. In this way, you will know instantly which fuse controls what line when you are doing any electrical wiring repairs or installations.

When a fuse blows, you should:

1. Turn off the master switch controlling the service conductors bring current into the house.

2. Remove the blown fuse and replace it with a 25-watt bulb to test the line.

3. Put the current on again. If the bulb burns dimly, the line is overloaded. This means that some appliances should be disconnected. It is a sign that you should have a new line added to carry the extra load normally required.

4. If the bulb burns brightly, there is a short circuit somewhere in the line. If you have a helper to watch the bulb, you can go the line and unscrew or turn off the lights on that circuit and disconnect any appliance. Do one at a time; when the test bulb goes out, you have found your trouble.

5. Leave the appliance disconnected or the switch off and put in a new fuse. Turn the main switch on again.

6. If the fuse blows again imme-

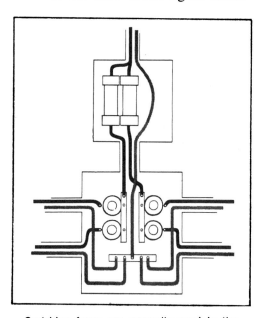

Cartridge fuses are normally used in the service entrance box to control the main electrical lines. The screw-in glass fuses are used as safety devices to control the branch circuits.

735

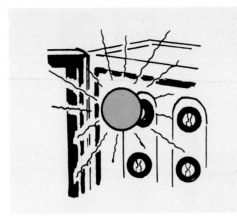

Sketch from "How To Do It Safely,"
Courtesy of The Home Insurance Co.

Use a 25-watt bulb to test the line when a
fuse blows.

Keep a list posted to the inside of the
fuse box showing the switches, light fixtures and outlets each fuse controls.

diately after you have screwed it in place, your difficulty may be more serious. There may be another short in the line caused by an appliance, switch or light, or there may be a short in the line itself. Here is where you can use professional help.

7. If nothing happens to the fuse, it is necessary to correct the short in the appliance, switch or lamp socket at a convenient time. Remember to shut off the current if it's necessary to replace a switch or fixture socket.

One note of caution: do not change fuses in the dark! Keep a flashlight handy near the fuse box for just such emergencies.

Wires in the Branch Circuits

When wiring branch circuits, it is best not to put all the lights and outlets in any one room on the same circuit. If that fuse were to blow you'd have no source of current in the room. Frequently, local wiring regulations require that ceiling lights and wall outlets be installed on separate circuits.

Here are the recommended sizes

736

of wire to use in different parts of the home:

1. For room lighting circuits—for ceiling or wall fixtures, portable lamps, radio, TV and movable appliances, such as a vacuum cleaner, use 2-wire #14 or #12.

2. For an electric range, use 3-wire #6 cable and protect each of the 'hot' or black wires with a 30 ampere fuse.

3. For the kitchen appliances—refrigerator, mixer, toaster, grill, etc., use 2-wire #10 cable protected by a 20-ampere fuse.

4. If you have a water heater operating on the electrical circuit, you should have a 2-wire #12 cable protected by a 20-ampere fuse.

5. If you have an electrically operated clothes dryer, use 3-wire #6 or #8 cable and protect the two black wires when the unit is operated on 220 volts with two fuses.

6. If you have a substantial number of power tools, it is best to use a separate circuit to the workshop; use 2-wire #10 cable protected by a 20-ampere fuse.

What Size Wire To Use

The size or diameter of the wire determines the electrical load it will carry just as the diameter of a pipe determines the amount of water it will permit to flow through. A thin wire carrying a heavy load will overheat; this will waste current in addition to being dangerous. The amount of current the wire will deliver will not be sufficient for the motor to run or the bulbs to light at top efficiency.

Every wire has a maximum allowable current-carrying capacity as shown in the accompanying table. In addition, the longer the wire, the greater the current loss or voltage drop. Therefore, it is necessary to plan your wiring so that you do not have an excessively long run for any one line. If, however, such a long run is necessary, it is essential to use a heavier or thicker wire, checking carefully the voltage drop of that wire.

The different types of wire given in the table "Maximum Current Carrying Capacity of Flexible Wires" are classes used by Underwriters' Laboratories to specify the type of insulation and covering over the wires. Generally, you will find this classification listed on the reel when you purchase wire, or it may be listed on a tag when the wire comes in a roll.

The diameter of the wire increases as the number designation gets smaller. A #18 wire is lighter or smaller than a #10.

Voltage drop is a vital consideration if you are running any power tools in your house. If the wire fails to deliver the proper voltage to your motor, not only with the power tool fail to work at top performance but your motor will burn out quickly. In the accompanying table is a guide showing the distance in feet which

MAXIMUM CURRENT CARRYING CAPACITY OF FLEXIBLE WIRES				
Size of Wire (Number)	Rubber Type*	Heavey Rubber or Thermoplastic** (amperes)	Asbestos****	Heavy Asbestos***
18	5	7	10	17
16	7	10	15	22
14	15	15	20	28
12	20	20		36
10	25	25		47
8	35			
6	45			
4	60			
2	80			

* Types PO, C, PD, PWP, K, E and ED
** Types S, SO, SJ, SJO, SV, POSJ, ST, STT, STV, and POT
*** Types HC, HPD and HSJ
**** Types AVPO and AVPD

	DISTANCE (IN FEET)					
AMPERES	#14	#12	#10	#8	#6	#4
1	450	700	1100	1800	2800	4500
2	222	350	550	900	1400	2200
3	150	240	350	600	900	1500
4	110	175	275	450	700	1100
5	90	140	220	360	560	880
10	45	70	110	180	280	450
15	30	45	70	120	180	300
20		35	55	90	140	225
30			35	60	90	150
40				45	70	110
60					45	75

different types of wire will carry a 110-volt current of different amperage with less than a 2% voltage drop.

Working with Wires

The first step in good electrical wiring is to know the right and the wrong way to make wire connections. In joining two or more wires, two essential requirements must be met. First, the wires must be bright and clean before they are joined. Secondly, the connection must be tight—either well fastened with solder and covered with tape or joined with solderless connectors.

Here is a guide for the handyman for cutting, splicing and connecting wires. Remember, joining the ends of two separate wires is known as a splice. Joining a wire at right angles to a continuous wire is called a tap.

When removing the insulation from a wire, it is best to cut at a slant as in sharpening a pencil. Expose about ½″ to ¾″ of the copper conductor. When removing the insulation, be careful not to scrape off the tin coating usually found on the wire; this tin coating makes soldering easier.

738

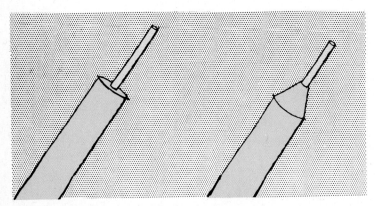

Solderless connectors simplify the joining of wires.

When connecting wire to a screw terminal, bend the end of the wire into a loop to fit around the screw. Attach the loop in the direction in which the screw turns when it is tightened. This will hold the wire under the head of the screw. If inserted in the opposite direction, there is always a chance of the wire working loose as the screw is tightened.

A tap splice is the joining of one wire at right angles to a continuous wire. For connecting the end of one wire at a point on a continuous wire, remove the insulation from the end of that single wire. Also bare a section of the continuous wire. Wrap the continuous wire around the exposed length as tightly as possible, making certain that both wires are clean. Then solder and tape.

A splice is the joining of two separate wires. It is necessary to remove about 3" of insulation from each of the two wires. After making certain that the wires are clean, cross the wires about 1" from the insulation. Then make 6 to 8 turns, using your fingers, with each wire and tighten the twisted sections with pliers to produce a splice similar to that shown in the sketch.

All splices have to be soldered and then taped. Always heat the wires with a soldering iron or gun or a blowtorch, making certain not to melt the insulation. After the two wires have been properly soldered, wrap rubber tape around the splice. It is best to extend the tape about 1" to 2" on either side of the joining of the wires. The rubber tape is then covered with friction tape. The friction tape should be wound from the opposite direction. It is possible to cover the splice with plastic tape. This new tape need not be covered with friction tape, although it is required in some communities by the local electrical code.

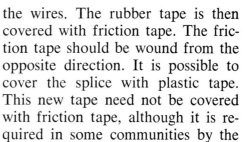

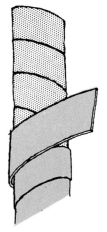

Solderless connectors eliminate the need for soldering the joining of wires. The connectors are made of an insulating material and once they are set over the wires, there is no possibility of shorting. Simply screw the connector over the two wires.

If both wires to be joined are solid, they are merely pressed closed together and the solderless connector is screwed over the two. On the other hand, if one is stranded and the other is a solid wire, it is better to twist the stranded wire around the solid wire in a clockwise direction and then screw the solderless connector over both. If you should wind the stranded wire around the solid one in the wrong direction, they will work loose as the solderless connector is screwed on. Should this happen, rewind the two wires at once and replace the connector.

Electrical Circuits

The electricity after leaving the main fuse box in your home goes through different branch circuits. Each of these circuits is capable of carrying electricity to specific outlets and lighting fixtures. Generally, a circuit in a home is designed to carry 15 amperes or to deliver about 2650 watts with normal 110-120 volts.

How effectively the electricity does its job depends upon the individual circuit. Probably the best way to explain electrical circuits is to use Christmas-tree lamps as an example.

Until recently, most Christmas-tree lights were connected by a single wire. There was a plug at one end and a single wire ran from bulb to bulb and finally returned to the plug. If one lamp was burned out or loose in the socket, none would light. These lamps were in *series*. Now, however, many Christmas-tree lamp cords are available where two wires run from socket to socket. These lamps are in *parallel*. The failure of one lamp will not affect the others. See the accompanying sketches for a visual explanation.

Wiring in series presents many problems. If any one item is not functioning, then the entire set won't work. A switch is wired in series with a light fixture. When the switch is 'off,' then the lamp is off; but if the switch is 'on,' the lamp burns brightly.

To make the individual parts in-

—•——SWITCH

—⊏▣⊐—OUTLET

BULB

A switch is always wired in series with the fixture or outlet it controls. Here the switch is wired in series with a lamp. When the switch is 'off,' the lamp is out; but when the switch is 'on,' the lamp lights.

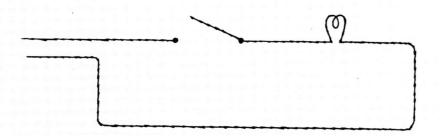

In this wiring diagram, the outlet is wired in parallel, but the switch and lamp are in series. The switch can be 'on' or 'off' and it will control only the lamp; the outlet will always have electricity available for use.

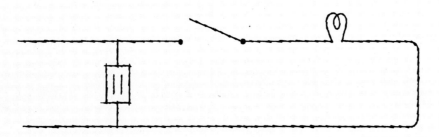

Although the lamp and outlet are wired in parallel in this circuit, the switch is in series with both. Thus if the switch is 'off,' neither the lamp nor the outlet will receive any electricity.

741

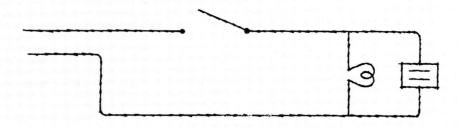

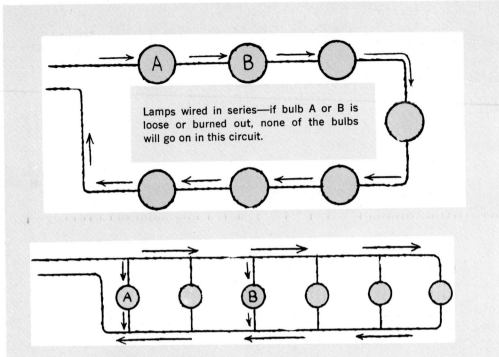

Lamps wired in series—if bulb A or B is loose or burned out, none of the bulbs will go on in this circuit.

Lamps wired in parallel—even if bulb A is burned out, bulb B as well as the others will light because current is available through the entire set of wires.

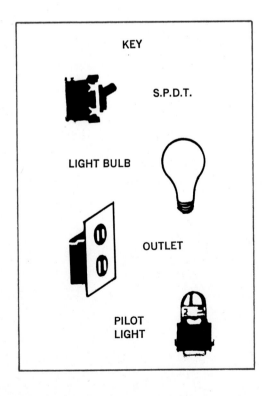

KEY

S.P.D.T.

LIGHT BULB

OUTLET

PILOT
LIGHT

742

dependent, outlets and lamps are wired in parallel. The flow of current remains uninterrupted even if one switch is 'off' or a lamp is burned out.

Common Wiring Diagrams

There are many wiring arrangements you can use inside and outside of your home. Here are several of the more common wiring diagrams to meet the need of the homeowner.

1. WALL SWITCH TO CONTROL CEILING LIGHT—If the wires from the fuse box reach the light fixture first, the black wire passes through the fixture box uninterrupted while the fixtures wires are connected in series with the white wire. Both the

black and white wires continue along the ceiling and down the wall to the switch. One wire is connected to each terminal. If you are using a mercury-type switch, make certain that it is positioned properly; one section is marked "top."

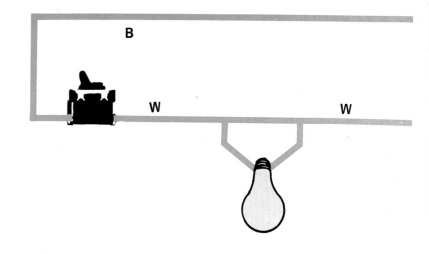

2. WALL SWITCH TO CONTROL CEILING LIGHT — The wires from the fuse box might come to the wall switch first. In this case, the black wire from the fuse box is connected to the switch. The black wire from the ceiling fixture is attached to the other terminal of the switch and the white wire from the ceiling light is joined to the white wire coming from the fuse box.

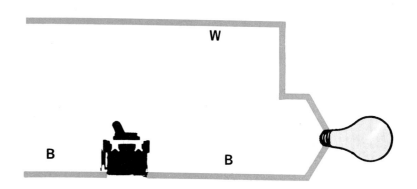

3. ONE SWITCH AND MORE THAN ONE CEILING LIGHT —A single wall switch can be used to control more than one light. All that is necessary is that the second light be wired in parallel. In this case the black wire from the second light is connected to the black wire from the switch and the black wire from the first light. The white wire from the second light joins the white wire of the first light and the white wire from the fuse box.

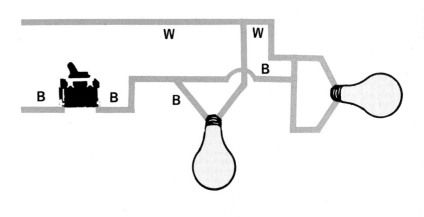

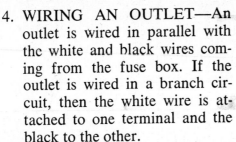

4. WIRING AN OUTLET—An outlet is wired in parallel with the white and black wires coming from the fuse box. If the outlet is wired in a branch circuit, then the white wire is attached to one terminal and the black to the other.

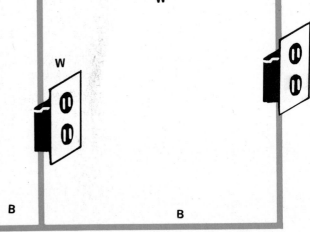

5. WIRING AN EXTRA OUTLET ON A LINE—To add an extra outlet to an existing outlet, it is necessary to wire it in parallel with the existing unit. Just run a black wire from the terminal connected to the black wire from the fuse box and add a white wire to the terminal from the fuse box.

744

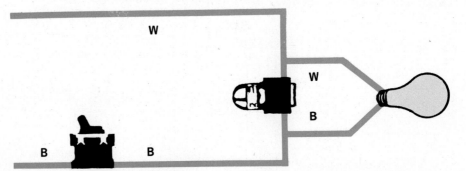

6. ADDING A PILOT LIGHT—Often you require a pilot light at the switch to indicate whether or not the light is on. This type of wiring circuit is sometimes found at the base of an attic stairway—the pilot light lets you know whether or not the attic light is on without your going up the stairs. The pilot light is wired in parallel with the light in the attic or wherever the light is that the switch controls.

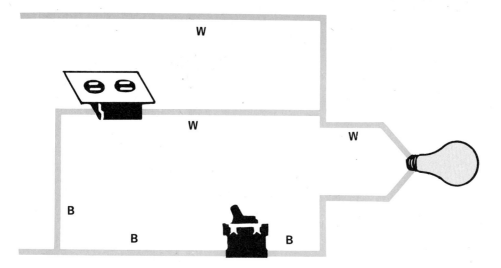

7. AN OUTLET WITH A SWITCH—Maybe you want an outlet next to the switch and to have the outlet work independent of that switch. This can be done easily if the wires from the fuse box come to the switch before the ceiling light. The outlet is wired in parallel with the wires from the fuse box before either wire is connected to the switch or ceiling light.

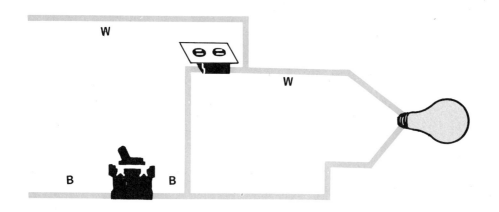

8. AN OUTLET WORKING OFF A SWITCH — Perhaps you'd prefer to have the outlet 'on' only when the switch and light are on. In this case, the outlet is again wired in parallel in the circuit, but it is connected after the switch. The current must flow through the switch before it reaches either outlet or the light. Outlet is controlled by switch.

745

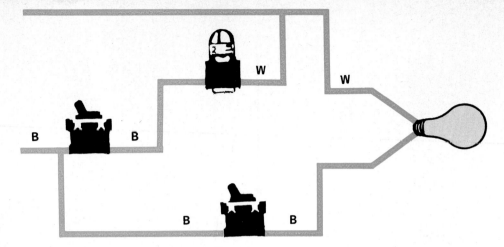

9. **SEPARATE NIGHT LIGHT ON A LINE**—In a child's room, a night light is a great convenience. It can be wired in to act independently of the regular room light. Two switches are needed—one controls the night light and the other the room light. Although complex looking, this wiring diagram is exceedingly simple. In consists of two series circuits: the switch and night light in one circuit and the other switch and room light in the other circuit. The wiring, however, is combined; the black wire from the fuse box is connected to one switch and then to the other by means of a jumper. The white wires from both the night light and room light are joined to the white wire from the fuse box.

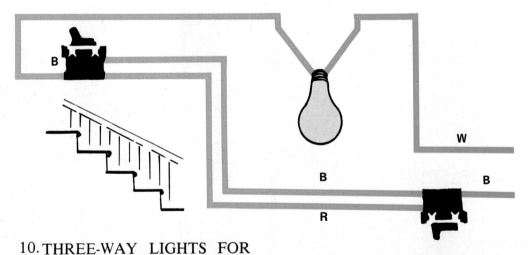

10. **THREE-WAY LIGHTS FOR STAIRWAYS**—To control a light from two different places, it is necessary to use a three-way switch. A three-wire cable is used between the two switches as each has three terminals. The red and black wires of the three-wire cable connect the two switches; the white wire is connected to the light. It is possible to have more than one light. However, all the lights have to be in parallel along the white wires between the two boxes.

Several lights can operate off a single circuit, but at least two lighting circuits should serve each room so that, if one should blow out, the room will not be in the dark.

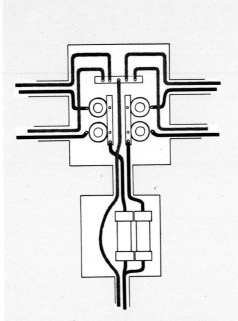

View of main fuse box showing two 110-volt lines plus a neutral line entering from the outside of the home and a fuse box with four branch circuits, each controlled by an individual fuse.

748

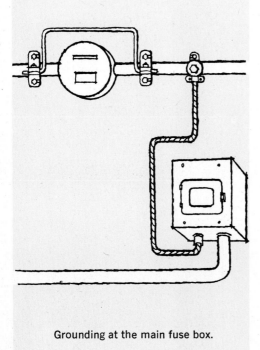

Grounding at the main fuse box.

The Main Fuse Box

All electrical wires come to you from the power company through a single service entrance switch. In many main fuse boxes, there is a single 'on-off' switch to control all the current. In homes without such a switch, the main fuse box has two cartridge fuse holders. A fuse is set across the main power line; removing this fuse shuts off the house current. Note that a fuse is wired in series. It is used only on the black line—the white line is the ground and there is no interruption in that line.

An electrical ground is any conductor that connects directly to the earth. It may, however, go through another conductor, such as a water pipe. Grounding the main fuse box is a must! It is required by the National Electrical Code and must be made in the prescribed manner.

Normally, a #4 or a #6 wire is used for grounding. This copper wire is heavy enough to be exposed, provided that the wire is free from danger of mechanical injury. If you should use a #8 wire, on the other hand, it must be of the armored type or else enclosed in a conduit.

The ground wire can be connected to the water pipe and a jumper provided to by-pass the water meter. You can also attach the ground wire to a copper rod, at least ½″ in diameter, or a steel or iron pipe, at least ¾″ in diameter. The rod or pipe must be at least 8′ long, and should be located at a minimum of 2′ from the building. The rod or pipe is driven into the earth so that at least 1′ to 2′ are underground. The ground wire is attached to the rod or pipe by means of a ground clamp, which connects the two firmly.

Wiring at the Main Box

In many homes two main conductors are brought to the fuse box although in some homes there are three wires. In the latter, two of the wires carry 110 volts and the third is the neutral or ground wire to complete the circuit. It is possible with this system to obtain 220 volts for operating an electric kitchen range, a motor or any other appliance, such as a dryer, on a 220-volt line.

The main conductors are protected upon entering the home by cartridge fuses. A separate cartridge fuse is used for each 110-volt line. In some communities, a glass 30-ampere fuse is used, while in other areas circuit breakers are permitted on the line. Note that no circuit breaker or fuse is used on the neutral or ground line.

After leaving the main fuse box, the electrical wires enter another box in which the branch lines or circuits are located. Some fuse boxes are large enough so that the main and branch fuse connections are in a single unit.

Generally, the main 'hot' leads are connected to the individual circuits through a receptacle into which a fuse is placed. A 15-ampere fuse is normally used for a branch circuit although a 20-ampere fuse is used for kitchen appliances as well as a washer in the laundry room. The neutral or ground wire is connected to a terminal board and there are taps (screws in a metal plate) which are numbered to correspond to the individual branch circuits.

To Add Additional Branch Circuits

If the main fuse box is capable of delivering the required power, it is possible to add additional branch circuits. This is often necessary when you add a freezer or a washer and prefer a separate circuit for these appliances. However, you cannot add extra circuits if your main fuse box is already carrying its maximum load.

A new fuse box is anchored near

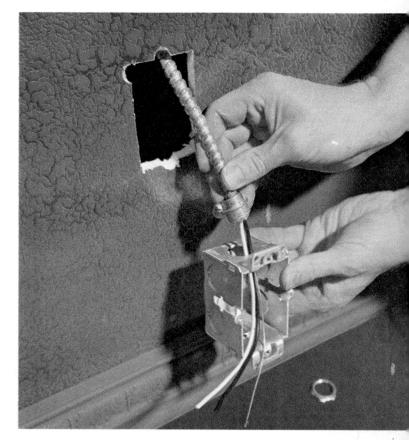

All wiring connections must be made inside a metal box, such as this outlet box.

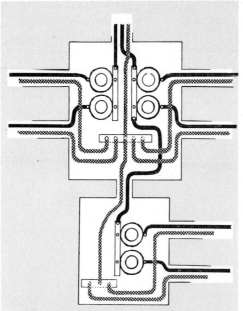

Adding an extra fuse box—note that the 'hot' lead is attached to one of the main or black wires in the main fuse box and another wire (usually white) is attached to the neutral bar in the main box. You must be extra careful when making a circuit connection of this type! The current in the main line is on unless you have pulled the main switch or removed the controlling fuses. Always do this before you start the wiring.

nected to the new fuse box and wired in a manner similar to the main fuse box.

Running Wires Through Walls

When adding new outlets or switches to control overhead lights, it is best to run the wires in the cavity between the inner and outer walls. You can use Romex or BX cable, depending upon the requirements in your local community.

To bring a cable up into the wall from the basement, it is necessary to drill a hole between two joists through the plate on which the wall rests. Make all measurements care-

the current main fuse box, although it is possible to place it anywhere inside the home you may wish. It is best to locate it near the present one because then you have all the major electrical controls in one place, in case something goes wrong and you have to test the circuits.

You will find a tap on one of the main current bars inside the main fuse box. If there isn't one in your box (point A in the accompanying sketch), you can connect a wire to the bar where another fuse is anchored. Attach a second wire, which will be the neutral of the new line, to the neutral bar in the main fuse box.

These two wires are then con-

750

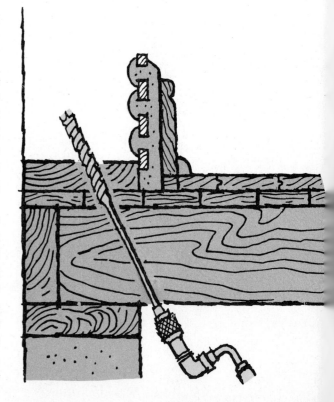

fully so that you drill the hole properly; you cannot afford to make a mistake and come up in the middle of a room. A brace with an extension bit or an electric drill with a bit extension and drill bit can be used to make the hole for the cable. Remember to make this hole large enough for the cable to slip through freely. It is not good policy to yank the cable through a small hole and possibly fray the insulated covering.

In some cases, it may be more convenient to draw the wire down from the attic into the wall cavity. This is particularly true in the second floor of a house or a house without a basement. Here it is necessary to drill through the top plate of the wall and to make the opening between two wall studs. An extension bit with a brace or an electric drill will make the job of drilling easy. Always check before drilling to make certain that the opening is made within the wall and not in the ceiling of a room.

Adding to an Existing Line

There are times when you wish to add only a single outlet in an existing line. Remember: all cable connections must be made within a switch, outlet or junction box. Merely cutting the cable and adding a branch to it cannot be done—there just isn't enough cable available to make proper connections. Here is what you have to do:

1. Shut off the power in the line.

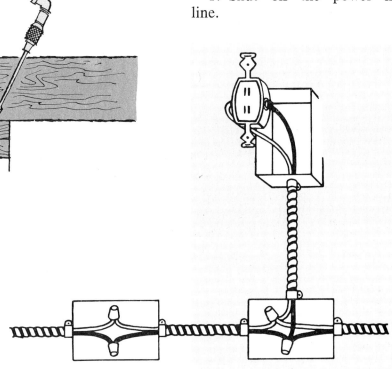

Complete view of wiring to show branch outlet added to a line.

2. Cut through the cable—the exterior insulated covering and both wires.

3. Two junction boxes are added in the line; see accompanying sketches.

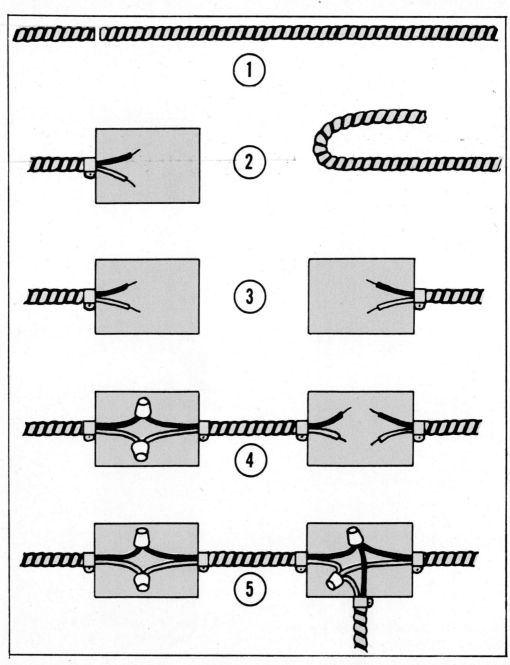

752

Here is how to add a branch in an existing line: (1) cut through the cable, both the insulation and the wires, (2) attach one end of the cut wire with a connector to a junction box, (3) about a foot or so away, attach the other wire to a junction box, (4) cut a piece of cable to join both boxes and connect it with the wires coming from the power supply, (5) add the branch wire to the outlet to the other junction box and join the wires within the box as shown.

4. A piece of cable connects the two boxes.

5. The new branch is connected within one of these boxes.

How to Replace a Switch

Replacing a switch or an outlet is very easy. However, before you start the job, shut off the power to that switch! Here is all you have to do:

1. Shut off the main switch or remove the fuse controlling the branch circuit on which the switch is located. If in doubt, pull the main switch—you can't afford to take chances!

2. Using a screwdriver, take off the cover plate. There are two small screws on either side of the switch handle. If you are changing a double outlet, you will generally find one screw in the center which holds the plate over the outlet.

3. Remove the plate and expose the switch inside the box in the wall. Set the plate and the two screws that hold the plate aside, preferably in a large ash tray or dish so that you won't loose any of the parts.

4. With a screwdriver, remove the screws holding the switch in the box. There are two screws, top and bottom, that go through holes in the switch ends into tapped holes in the box. An outlet is held in a box in the same manner.

5. With the two screws removed and safely put away, pull the switch out of the box as far as the wires will permit. Avoid pulling too hard because you may break the wires if they are old.

6. With a screwdriver, loosen the terminal screws holding the wires to the switch. Be careful when

1. Remove switch plate with screwdriver.

2. With the cover plate off and the current off, remove the switch from the box by removing the two screws that hold the switch in place.

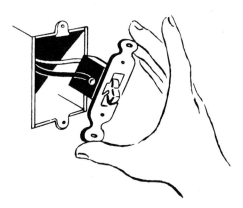

3. Pull the switch and the wires out of the box as far as you can, taking care not to break the wires.

4. Remove the wires by loosening the terminal screws. The new switch is replaced by following the directions in reverse.

753

working with solid wire for it may snap.

7. Clean the ends of the two wires and set them under the terminal screws of a new switch. The black wire is placed under one of the terminal screws and the white wire under the other terminal screw. Tighten the screws with a screwdriver.

8. Push the wires and switch back into the box so that the holes in the ends of the switch line up with the holes in the switch box. Replace the two screws that hold the switch in the box.

9. Replace the fuse and test the light, being careful not to touch any of the wires or terminals in the box. If the light switch works, remove the fuse again.

10. Now replace the switch plate and tighten the two screws that hold it in place. Be careful not to tighten too much if you have a plastic or glass plate for you are liable to crack it.

11. With the plate in place, replace the fuse and the job is completed.

Electric Appliance Cords

The cords by which electrical appliances are connected to a circuit often cause trouble. In most cases, this is due either to wear or to improper handling, but in some cases may be the result of moisture, oil, or heat.

A cord usually shows the first signs of wear at the point where it is most frequently handled or where bends occur. If the cord is twisted often and bent sharply, the stranded wire beneath the covering may break and perforate the insulation.

If it comes into contact with a conductor of the opposite polarity, a short circuit will result, causing a flash or arc which may start a fire. Even if the insulation is not perforated, the failure of the small constituent wire of such a conductor will ultimately result in reduced current to the device, perhaps with a 'hot spot' in the conductor. When all of the small wires in a conductor have failed, the current cannot flow through it, and the appliance will not work. Defective cords should be promptly discarded.

When disconnecting an appliance from a plug, the cap should be grasped to avoid pulling on the cord. This will prevent strain on the wires. Some caps are obtainable with handles attached. If a cord becomes badly damaged, it should be replaced. However, if the cord is sound and has merely been pulled out of the plug, it can readily be reconnected.

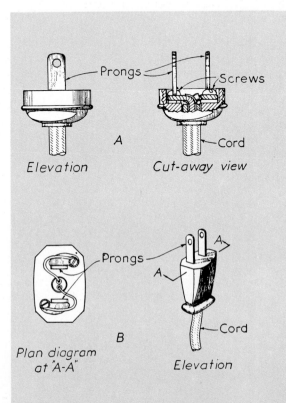

Prongs — Screws — Cord

A

Elevation — Cut-away view

Prongs — Cord

B

Plan diagram at "A-A" — Elevation

REPLACING CORD IN PLUG

Clip the end of the cord and push it through the hole in the cap from the outer side. Next, split and remove the outside braid of the cord for about 1″ from the end, which will expose the two separately covered wires within. Carefully remove the insulation from these wires for a distance of ½″.

Twist the strands of each wire to keep them together and form each of the conductors into a loop so that the wire runs in a clockwise direction when placed under the terminal screw. Then loop each wire around the blades of the plug, and secure under the terminal screws.

Caution: Make sure there are no bare wires of opposite polarity to come into contact with each other!

Various special types of plugs are now available that require even less work to connect. Some merely clamp on the ends of the wires in such a way as to pierce the insulation and make the connections automatically.

When the cord becomes too worn, it ought to be discarded and replaced with a cord, which is approved by the Underwriters' Laboratories for the specific use for which it is intended.

UNDERWRITERS' KNOT

A special method of securing the wire in a plug is recommended—it is called an Underwriters' knot. It is designed to prevent the pulling out of the wires from the plug if the cord is inadvertently jerked while it is connected to the outlet.

Just follow the accompanying sketches to tie the knot. It is best

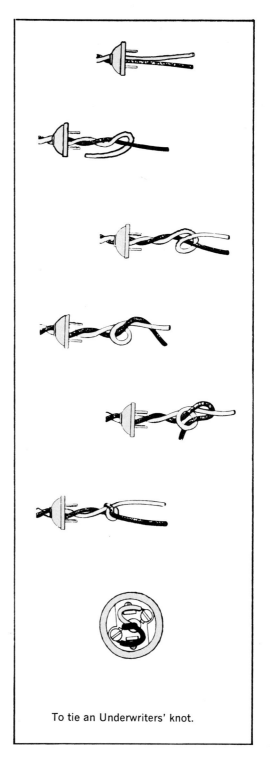

To tie an Underwriters' knot.

to pull about 3″ of wire through the plug for the knot and then cut off the excess.

SPLICING CORD

As previously emphasized, when a cord is badly worn, it is best to replace it with a new one. However, for emergency or temporary measure you may want to splice a cord which is broken, or perhaps lengthen a cord you now find too short.

The procedure is to scrape the two wire ends (which are to be connected) clean; use a knife for the purpose. It may be necessary to sandpaper the two wire ends if they aren't very smooth. The scraped, clean areas of the two wires should extend about 3″ from the ends. Bring the two wires together, about 2″ from the ends, and cross them over. Then, with the end of each wire, make about 5 or 6 turns until there is a secure fastening. Snip the two ends off with a pair of pliers, and squeeze them tightly to make certain there are no sharp protrusions to penetrate the outer covering. Solder the two ends and cover with rubber and friction tapes, made especially for electrical purposes.

Electric Sockets

A pull chain or key controls a push bar for the switch within the socket. If necessary to make repairs to the socket, it must be taken apart. Turn off current before starting! Use a screwdriver to pry apart the upper part of the socket; you will see where dents are made for the upper part to fit over the lower, and it is by pushing up on the dents that you can separate the two parts.

Inside the socket you will find the terminal screws where the switch mechanism is connected. Loosen these screws, then remove the defective switch, and replace with a new one by connecting it to the wires. The two wires are inserted through the socket cap. Tie the two wire ends with a double knot (called an Underwriter's knot); there are two reasons for this: it relieves strain of the weight on the connection, and it enables the wire ends to fit tightly into the socket cap.

When the two wires are knotted, with a knife scrape off the outer covering on the ends of the two wires. Then attach the two wire ends to the terminal screws; wind the wire around the screws in a clockwise direction. Now tighten the screws, snip off loose wire ends. Replace the fiber insulating shell, and finally put on the outer metal shell, being sure the upper and lower part fit very securely at the dents where they meet.

Connecting a cord to a lamp socket
a. Bushing with screw
b. Cap
c. Porcelain or bakelite socket base
d. Paper shell
e. Brass shell

Trouble-Shooting Fluorescents

Many homes use fluorescent lights since they provide three times as much illumination as a filament lamp consuming the same wattage. Generally, a fluorescent lamp will last from 2500 to 3000 hours and will warn you as it approaches its end by flashing on and off.

There are times when the lamp does not work effectively even before it is due to burn out. Here are some symptoms and cures for faulty fluorescent lamps.

1. The lamp flickers for several seconds before it finally goes on.—There is a voltage drop either in the supply of current to the home or a loss along the individual circuit in the home. Check to see if there is too much of a load on the circuit.

2. The ends of the tube darken while the bulb is still new.—The current has been exceeding 110-115 volts because of faulty power regulation at the generating plant. Sometimes reversing the fluorescent tube will correct this difficulty. If, however, the power fluctuation from the power company varies too greatly, it may be necessary to forget about fluorescent bulbs in your home.

3. The bulb burns out rapidly. —You may have been using an incorrect starter with the bulb. Take out the starter and check to see if it is of the type recommended for the fluorescent bulb you are using.

WHEN THE LIGHT WON'T GO ON

If you turn on the switch and the fluorescent bulb won't go on, you should follow this procedure:

1. Check other lights on the same circuit to see that current is flowing in the line.

2. If there is current in the line and the bulb doesn't go on, replace the starter.

3. Should the bulb still fail to go on, remove the fluorescent tube and check the contact points at the end. They may be dirty and should be sanded lightly.

4. Replace the bulb and try again.

5. If the light doesn't go on, shut off the power to that circuit by removing the fuse.

6. Check the contact points in the fixture. They may be bent or corroded. Sand the contact points or straighten them, if bent.

7. Should the lamp not go on after it is replaced in the fixture and the current turned on, then remove the fuse again.

8. With the current off, remove the fixture and check the wiring inside to make certain that all connections are properly made.

9. Test the switch by removing it and checking it with a test light in your workshop. The switch may be faulty and, if it is, replace it.

10. If the switch is working, then the ballast inside the fixture is probably at fault and a new one should be substituted.

If you have checked carefully as you worked along, you should be able to replace the entire unit, set the bulb in the sockets and turn on the current. The job will be completed.

How to Read an Electric Meter

Most electric meters have four dials which resemble clocks. They

757

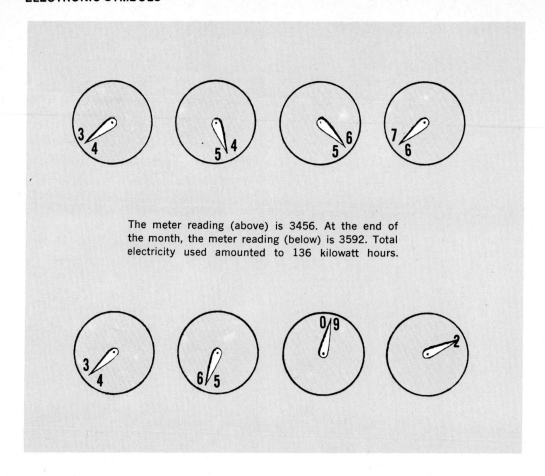

The meter reading (above) is 3456. At the end of the month, the meter reading (below) is 3592. Total electricity used amounted to 136 kilowatt hours.

are numbered from 0 through 9 instead of 1 through 12 like a clock. Each clock has only one hand and in two of the clocks, the numbers are read counter-clockwise.

To read your meter, mark down the reading and a month later copy the reading again. Let's assume that the reading shown in the accompanying sketch is that taken at the beginning of the month.

• It is 3456.

The reading at the end of the month as shown in the sketch is:

• 3592, the last reading.

The difference between these two is 136. In other words, you have consumed 136 kilowatt hours of electricity during the month.

Electronic Symbols

Here are some of the symbols which are standard in radio, TV and electronic diagrams. The popular component parts are shown according to industry-wide agreement in labeling of the parts.

Note that two methods of wire connection and crossover are included in this list of symbols. While both are in common use, the preferred method to show a connection

758

Electronic Schematic Symbols

	ANTENNA (BROADCAST)		AIR CORE TRANSFORMER (RF)		CRYSTAL DETECTOR
	ANTENNA (TV, FM)		IRON CORE TRANSFORMER (AF)		RECTIFIER
	ANTENNA (LOOP)		I.F. TRANSFORMER (DOUBLE TUNED)		PILOT LAMP
	GROUND		POWER TRANSFORMER		HEADPHONES
	CHASSIS CONNECTION		P – 115 VOLT PRIMARY		LOUDSPEAKER PM DYNAMIC
	WIRING Method 1 CONNECTION		S1 – CENTER-TAPPED SECONDARY FOR FILAMENTS OF SIGNAL CIRCUIT TUBES		LOUDSPEAKER ELECTRODYNAMIC
	NO CONNECTION		S2 – SECONDARY FOR RECTIFIER TUBE FILAMENT		PHONO PICK-UP
	WIRING Method 2 CONNECTION		S3 – CENTER-TAPPED HIGH-VOLTAGE SECONDARY		
			FIXED CONDENSER (MICA OR PAPER)		VACUUM TUBE FILAMENT
	NO CONNECTION		FIXED CONDENSER (ELECTROLYTIC)		VACUUM TUBE CATHODE
	"A" BATTERY, OR SINGLE CELL		VARIABLE CONDENSER		VACUUM TUBE GRID
	"B" BATTERY, OR MULTI-CELL		GANG TUNING CONDENSER		VACUUM TUBE PLATE
	RESISTOR		POWER SWITCH S.P.S.T.		3-ELEMENT VACUUM TUBE
	POTENTIOMETER (VOLUME CONTROL)		SWITCH S.P.D.T.		TUBE GAS FILLED
	RHEOSTAT		SWITCH D.P.D.T.		ALIGNING KEY OCTAL BASE TUBE
	AIR CORE COIL (OR CHOKE)		SWITCH D.P.S.T.		METER
	IRON CORE COIL (OR CHOKE)		SWITCH ROTARY OR SELECTOR		A – AMMETER MA – MILLIAMMETER MA – MICROAMMETER V – VOLTMETER W – WATTMETER G – GALVANOMETER
	IRON CORE COIL PERMEABILITY TUNED		FUSE		MICROPHONE

759

Chart courtesy of Allied Radio Corporation.

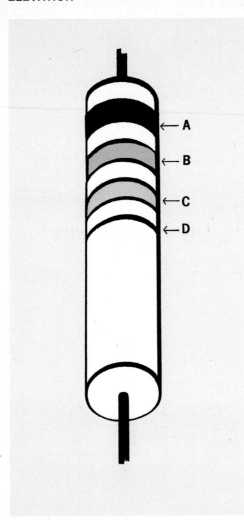

is with the dot in method 1, while the preferred method of showing a crossover or no connection between the wire is the simple crossing of the lines, also shown in method 1.

The symbol for the ground point may indicate an actual connection to the metal chassis of the unit or a connection to a ground lead, usually the B— voltage point. All ground points may usually be assumed to be connected together electrically.

Color Code For Resistors

All carbon resistors are produced and color-coded to meet the standards set up by the RETMA (Radio, Electronics and Television Manufacturers' Association). Here is your guide to resistors by color bands.

Elevation

This term is used to describe a drawing to scale showing the up-

760

Color-Code Chart							
Band A		**Band B**		**Band C**		**Band D**	
Color	Value	Color	Value	Color	Value	Color	Tolerance
Black	0	Black	0	Black	None	None	±20%
Brown	1	Brown	1	Brown	0	Silver	±10%
Red	2	Red	2	Red	00	Gold	± 5%
Orange	3	Orange	3	Orange	000		
Yellow	4	Yellow	4	Yellow	0000		
Green	5	Green	5	Green	00000		
Blue	6	Blue	6	Blue	000000		
Violet	7	Violet	7	Violet	0000000		
Gray	8	Gray	8	Gold	÷10		
White	9	White	9	Silver	÷100		

Note: The first band (A) shows the first figure of the resistor value, the second band (B) shows the second figure, and the third band (C) indicates the number of zeros to be added. The fourth band (D), which is not included in all resistors, merely indicates the tolerance. If the last band (D) is omitted, the tolerance of the resistor is plus or minus 20%.

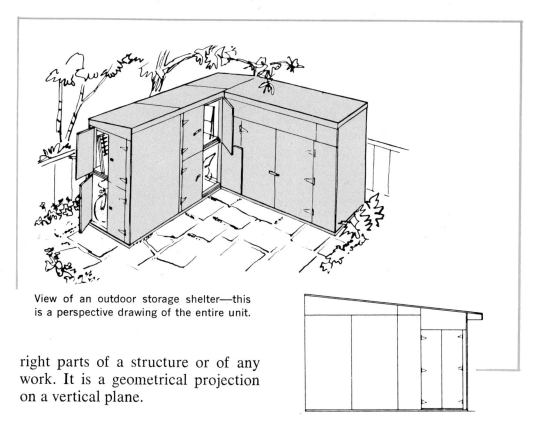

View of an outdoor storage shelter—this is a perspective drawing of the entire unit.

This is the rear elevation—a view from the back of unit taken from the far right-hand corner in the perspective drawing.

right parts of a structure or of any work. It is a geometrical projection on a vertical plane.

Emery Cloth

Powdered emery is an abrasive made of corundum composed of oxide of alumina, iron, silica and a small portion of lime. It is glued to a thin cloth and is used for removing file marks on metal and for polishing metallic surfaces.

Also see *ABRASIVES*.

Enamel

This is applied as a finish to the surface of wood and metal, in the same manner as paint, either with a brush or a spray. The finish produced by coating with enamel is glossy, or sometimes flat, depending on the type used. In interior decoration it is used more in the nature of a 'trim' and for cabinets and furniture, rather than as a finish for large wall areas, except in kitchens and bathrooms where it is used for moisture resistance and washability.

Enamel is available in a heat-proof quality, as a finish for metal radiators, heating grilles, exposed water pipes, and stoves. The variety of colors in which enamel may be purchased gives it a wide range for any interior decorating scheme, either on wood or metal surfaces.

Also see *PAINTING*.

761

End-Grain

The face or edge of a piece of wood exposed when its fibers are cut transversely. End-grain requires special treatment when finishing.

If the end-grain is to be painted, it should be filled with a wood filler which, when dry is sanded smooth.

If the end-grain is to be stained, it is often best to apply a very thin coat of shellac or resin sealer over

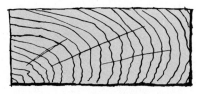

the surface. In this way, the stain will not penetrate deeply into the fibers and make the edge or end-grain darker than the rest of the surface.

End-Lap Joint

This is a corner joint formed by halving both pieces of wood for a distance equal to their widths.

An end-lap can be cut with hand tools by cutting through half

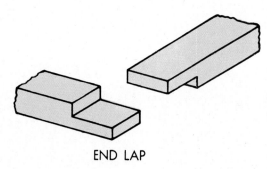

END LAP

Two pieces already cut to form a corner-end lap joint.

the thickness of each piece with a backsaw and then cutting at right angles so that equal pieces are removed from both pieces of wood to be joined.

The end-lap can also be cut with a power saw. Either you can make a series of parallel cuts through half the thickness of the wood and remove the excess with a chisel, or you can use a dado blade to remove the required portion of each piece.

End-lap joints can be fastened with adhesive, nails or screws, or a combination of adhesive and nails or adhesive and screws.

Also see *JOINTS*.

Entryway

A house which lacks a vestibule, where the door opens directly outdoors, will be greatly improved by the addition of a closed-in or a shielded entryway. Whether the door is flush with the ground level or raised over a small stoop of a few stairs, an enclosure or shield can be added to keep the rain from driving in when the door is opened.

Colorful reinforced plastic panels can be utilized to make such enclosures. These plastic panels are translucent and shatterproof and can be sawed, nailed and drilled just like wood.

Available in deep and pastel colors as well as white—both flat and corrugated—the panels admit light but maintain privacy. Furthermore, the panels are permanently colored and require no finishing or repainting.

Also see *CANOPY*.

762

SIDEWALL AND CANOPY

An eggcrate pattern is used for the roof and is covered with plastic Fiberglas. The side wall is made of a wooden frame of 2x2's with flat plastic sheets set inside the wooden framework. A brick or stone planter along the base adds to the decorative appearance. For cutting the framing for the canopy, see **Eggcrate** section under **Furniture.**

Sketches courtesy of Monsanto Chemical Co.

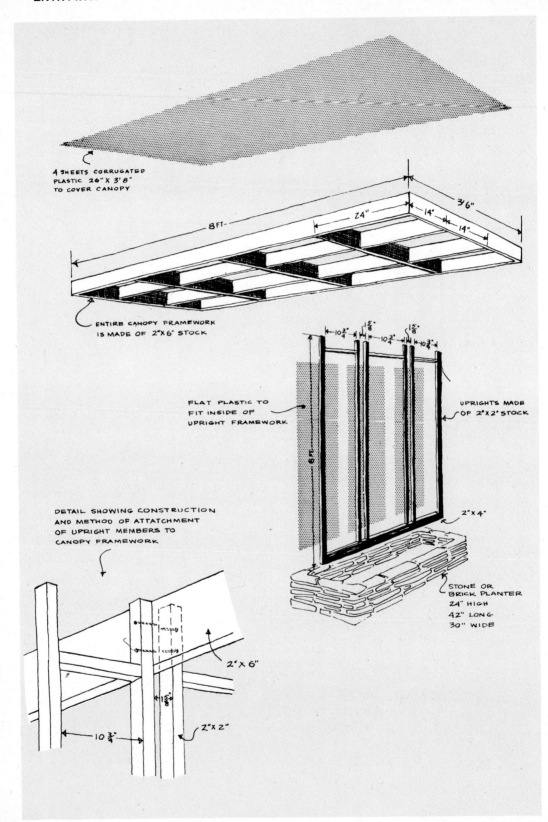

4 SHEETS CORRUGATED
PLASTIC 26" X 3'8"
TO COVER CANOPY

3'6"

8FT.

24"

14"

14"

ENTIRE CANOPY FRAMEWORK
IS MADE OF 2"X6" STOCK

10¾"

1⅝"

10¾"

1⅝"

10¾"

FLAT PLASTIC TO
FIT INSIDE OF
UPRIGHT FRAMEWORK

UPRIGHTS MADE
OF 2"X2" STOCK

6 FT.

2"X4"

DETAIL SHOWING CONSTRUCTION
AND METHOD OF ATTATCHMENT
OF UPRIGHT MEMBERS TO
CANOPY FRAMEWORK

STONE OR
BRICK PLANTER
24" HIGH
42" LONG
30" WIDE

2"X6"

1⅝"

10¾"

2"X2"

764

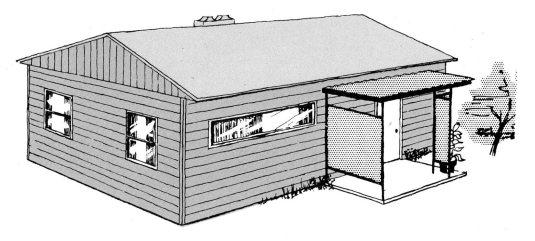

TWIN WALL-CANOPY ENTRYWAY

Here's a way to make the concrete slab in front of your door more interesting. Sun shadow patterns from this entry treatment give a plain house a 'lift.' Wall framing is made of 4x4's with angle irons used to attach uprights to concrete slab. Eggcrate design of 2x6's is used for the canopy.

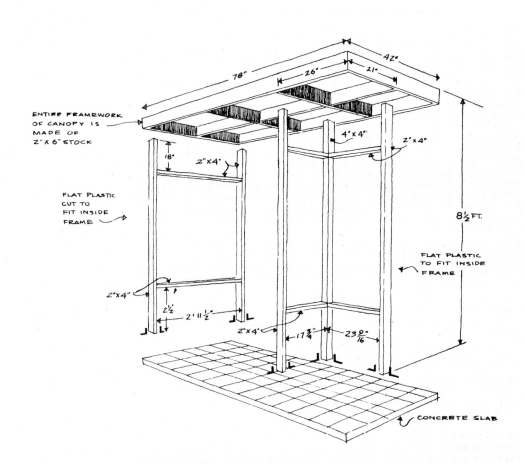

765

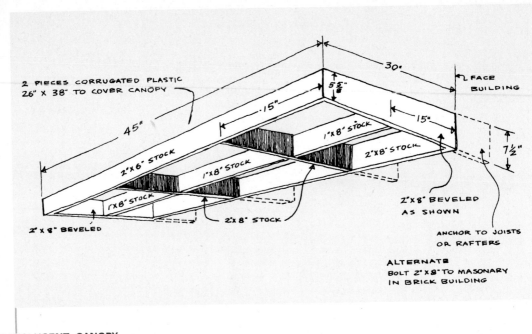

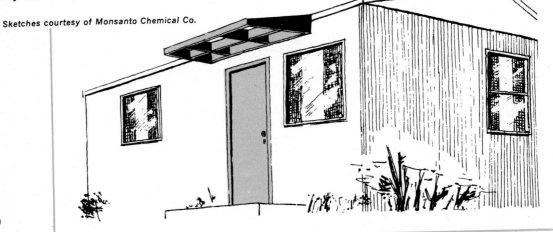

TRANSLUCENT CANOPY

Keep the rain out with modern overhang. The eggcrate frame is secured to the house exterior with lag screws in lead anchors or Rawl plugs, or with screws directly into the studs.

Sketches courtesy of Monsanto Chemical Co.

766

Equivalents, Weights and Measures

The metric system of weights and measures long in use in most parts of the world, is almost certain to be adopted in the United States within the next several years. Regardless of whether or when that may happen, it is helpful to understand the relationship of the system of ounces, inches and quarts to that of grams, meters and liters.

Capacity Tables (Liquid)

a. U. S. Liquid Measure
8 fluid drams (fl dr)
= 1 fluid ounce (fl oz).
4 fluid ounces   = 1 gill.
4 gills   = 1 pint (pt).
2 pints   = 1 quart (qt).
4 quarts   = 1 gallon (gal).
    = 231 cubic inches.

At maximum density, 39.164° F., a gallon of pure water weighs 8.345 pounds; at 59° F., the weight is 8.338 pounds.

b. Metric Capacity Measure
1,000 milliliters (ml) = 1 liter (l).
1,000 liters = 1 kiloliter (kl).
The term "cubic centimeter" has been commonly used instead of "milliliter." Technically, this is not correct, since the cubic centimeter is a measure of volume, not of capacity. For practical purposes, however, they may be regarded as equal.

c. Equivalents of Capacity
1 fluid ounce   =   29.5729 milliliters.
1 pint   = 473.167   milliliters.
1 gallon   =   3.7853 liters.
0.2705 fluid dram
    =   1   milliliter.
33.8147 fluid ounces
    =   1   liter.
1.0567 quarts   =   1   liter.

d. Equivalents for Teaspoonful, Tablespoonful, and Cup
3 teaspoonfuls   = 1 tablespoonful.
2 tablespoonfuls   = 1 fluid ounce.
16 tablespoonfuls   = 1 cup.
8 fluid ounces   = 1 cup.
15 milliliters   = 1 tablespoonful.
1 pint   = 2 cups.

Area-Measurement Tables

a. U. S. System
144 square inches
    (sq in) = 1 square foot (sq ft)
9 square feet
    = 1 square yard (sq yd).
30¼ square yards
    = 1 square rod (sq rd).
43,560 square feet
    = 1 acre.

b. Metric System
100 square millimeters
    = 1 square centimeter.
100 square centimeters
    = 1 square decimeter.
100 square decimeters
    = 1 square meter.
100 square meters = 1 are.
100 ares   = 1 hectare.

c. Equivalents of Area
1 square inch
    = 6.452   square centimeter.
1 square foot
    = 9.2903 square decimeter.
1 square yard
    = 0.8361 square meter.
1 acre   = 0.4047 hectare.
0.155   square inch
    = 1 square centimeter.
1.1960 square yards
    = 1 square meter.
2.471   acres = 1 hectare.

767

Weight Tables

a. U. S. Avoirdupois Weight

$27\frac{11}{32}$ grains (gr)	= 1 dram (dr.)
16 drams	= 1 ounce (oz).
16 ounces	= 1 pound (lb).
	= 7,000 grains.
2,000 pounds	= 1 short ton.

b. Metric Weight

1,000 micrograms	= 1 milligram (mg).
1,000 milligrams	= 1 gram (gm).
1,000 grams	= 1 kilogram (kg).
1,000 kilograms	= 1 metric ton.

c. Equivalent of Weight

1 ounce	=	28.3495 grams.
1 pound	=	453.59 grams.
0.03527 ounce	=	1 gram.
2,2046 pounds,	=	1 kilogram

Volume (Cubic Measure) Tables

a. U. S. System

1,728 cubic inches (cu in)	= 1 cubic foot (cu ft).
27 cubic feet	= 1 cubic yard (cu yd).

b. Metric System

1,000 cubic millimeters	= 1 cubic decimeter.
1,000 cubic centimeters	= 1 cubic meter.
1,000 cubic decimeters	= 1 cubic centimeter.

c. Equivalents of Volume

1 cubic inch	=	16.39 cubic centimeters.
1 cubic foot	=	28.317 cubic decimeters.
1 cubic yard	=	0.7646 cubic meter.
0.061 cubic inch	=	1 cubic centimeter.
1.308 cubic yards	=	1 cubic meter.

Linear-Measure Tables

a. U. S. System

12 inches (in)	= 1 foot (ft).
3 feet	= 1 yard (yd).
$16\frac{1}{2}$ feet	= 1 rod (rd).
5,280 feet	= 1 mile.

b. Metric System

1,000 microns	= 1 millimeter (mm).
10 millimeters	= 1 centimeter (cm).
1,000 centimeters	= 1 meter (m).
1,000 meters	= 1 kilometer (km).

c. Equivalents of Length

1 inch	=	2.54 centimeters.
1 foot	=	30.48 centimeters.
1 mile	=	1.60935 kilometers.
0.3937 inch	=	1 centimeter.
39.37 inches	=	1 meter.
0.62137 mile	=	1 kilometer.

The expansion bit.

Expansion Bit

Also called an expansive bit, this is a boring tool which can be set to make varying diameter large holes in wood. The cutter, regulated by an adjusting screw, can be moved closer or farther away from the screw-tip point for boring the proper diameter hole.

Moving the cutter adjusting screw in some types of expansion bits automatically moves the cutter an exact amount. One complete turn of the screw of a Russell Jennings bit enlarges or reduces the hole ⅛″—a half turn, 1/16″.

It is best to test the size of the hole on a scrap piece of wood before doing the actual boring. Use a brace with the bit. It is always best to clamp a piece of waste wood on the back of the work to prevent splitting.

Sketch from "Tool Guide" courtesy of Stanley Tools.

Expansion bit used in wood.

Photograph courtesy of Reynold's Do-It-Yourself Aluminum.

Expansion bit is used to make large diameter holes with a brace. It is adjustable to within 1/64″. Note that a piece of waste wood is used to back up the thin aluminum—this facilitates the drilling. Woodworking tools may be used with this special type of aluminum.

769

Expansion Bolt

A bolt equipped with a split or hinged casing which acts as a wedge. As the bolt is screwed into

An expansion bolt.

the casing, the ends of the casing expand to form a wedge. This type of bolt is used as an anchor in brick or concrete.

Also see *ANCHORS FOR CONCRETE* and *BOLTS*.

Expansion Joint

When two masses are set next to each other and each is subject to expansion and contraction, a special joint is used between them. This joint is flexible, providing space for the mass to move into when it expands. It is flexible enough so that when the mass contracts, the joint expands to fill the gap.

Expansion joints are generally used when laying concrete. A space is left between two large sections of concrete (using a board treated with oil or grease, or a metal divider for easy removal after the concrete has set). This space is filled with asphalt which, while it hardens on the surface, remains pliable inside. Another method of adding an expansion joint is by using specially-treated felt and setting it between the masses of concrete as each section is formed.

If an expansion joint is not used with large masses of concrete, there is a good chance it will buckle and crack. Should this happen, it is necessary to chop openings for expansion joints and to repair the cracked concrete.

It is always best to use an expansion joint when laying a concrete

Expansion joints are provided between sections of the concrete walkway around this swimming pool, and between the walkway and the pool coping.

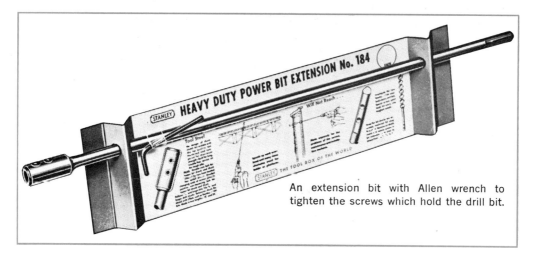

An extension bit with Allen wrench to tighten the screws which hold the drill bit.

patio abutting the house. This joint can be made by using a 1x4 set between the house and patio. While the wood can remain and act as a cushion, it will eventually rot. Therefore, remove it after the concrete is cured and pour asphalt into the opening.

Extension Bit

Often when using an electric drill, the bit is not long enough to penetrate through a wide piece of wood, or it is not possible to get the drill close enough to the work, for example, when drilling through a plate to run an electric cable in the wall. The extension bit has a ¼″ diameter end which fits into the drill chuck. On the other end is a circular opening into which the bit is fitted. The bit is held in the extension bit by means of two Allen screws.

For exceedingly long holes and hard-to-reach places, it is possible to join more than one extension bit to a drill. However, a certain amount of wobble develops and this is neither good for the drill nor for the work. The hole will be larger than the bit used if there is a wobble.

Eyebolt

When a bolt has a hole or an eye at one end of the usual head, it is classed as an eyebolt. The eye is used to receive a pin, stud, rope or hook.

Also see *BOLTS*.

An eyebolt has a hole or opening in one end and a threaded section with a nut at the other end.

771

Walls of this studio apartment are covered with a floral-patterned sheeting. Extra-wide width means fewer seams; hemmed edges mean that less finishing work is required. Seaming was accomplished with back-tacking (see text). Stationary draperies are of the same sheeting. Folding screens are also covered with fabric.

Fabric

Fabric is an ideal, easy-to-use material for the do-it-yourself decorator, who can apply it to furniture, picture frames, boxes, trunks, woodwork and even walls swiftly and simply with surprisingly professional-appearing results. Techniques are easily mastered, and include sewing, gluing and stapling. Several typical projects are shown here, but the beauty of working with fabric is that you are limited only by your own imagination in creating truly unique, customized effects.

Measuring and Cutting

Fabric covers a multitude of flaws that paint or even wallpaper often won't. It can be cotton or felt, stretch vinyl or double-knit, a blended printed sheet or almost any other material you'd like to decorate with. If the job is small, chances are a remnant will do. To determine yardage needed, first measure each section of the object to be covered, and mark these measurements on a piece of paper. When covering furniture or similar objects, allow for seams and for wrapping fabric around edges and corners; on large areas such as walls, allow for matching pattern.

Cut out paper patterns and lay on the fabric to determine most economical cutting. Then cut the fabric.

Fabric on Furniture

When covering furniture, remove hinges, knobs and other hardware before you begin. Staple or tack the fabric completely over one edge first, the opposite edge next, pulling the material taut but taking care not to stretch or distort it. Miter corners by folding fabric neatly around them, trimming away excess. When covering large, flat areas, white glue can be used to hold fabric tightly in place.

Fabric on Walls

To apply fabric to walls, nail or screw lathing strips up both ends of the wall, across the top and bottom, and around doors and windows; also, up the wall at intervals equal to the width of the fabric strips, minus 2″. Cut fabric to required lengths, allowing 1″ for turn-under above doors and windows.

Fold lengthwise edges of a fabric strip 1″ over a tacking strip, pushing the fabric firmly down over the tacks. Starting in a corner, staple the fabric to the top and bottom lathing strips. Hammer tacks in side folds into lathing strips. Repeat for as many panels as are needed, butting the vertical folded edges, and using tacking strips inside 1″ folds above doors and windows. Glue or tack molding on all stapled edges.

Back-Tacking

Back-tacking is the professional method of hiding staples while joining fabric sections smoothly. Place a fabric edge along the edge of the item to be covered (Fig. 1). Staple fabric edge at several points, then place upholsterer's tape or a ½″-wide strip of cardboard along the stapled edge. Staple through tape or cardboard and fabric (Fig. 2). Bring fabric over tape, right-side out (Fig. 3). Smooth fabric; staple the opposite edge. Repeat the back-tacking with the edge of the next fabric piece, overlapping the stapled edge of the first piece. Glue the final edge where it is not possible to hide the staples by back-tacking.

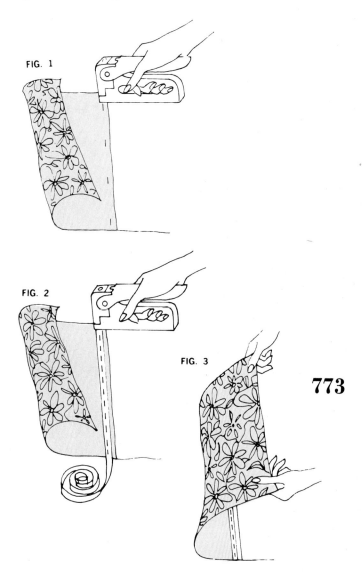

FIG. 1

FIG. 2

FIG. 3

773

This traditional room is literally swathed in polyester double-knit, one of the most popular fashion fabrics. Not only does knit cover the upholstered pieces, but draperies and even wallcovering are knits for a unique combination of colors, patterns and textures.

Print Your Own Designs

Using a linoleum cut, you can block-print your own designs on yardage (cotton, linen, muslin, poplin work beautifully) for slipcovers, floor cushions, pillows, curtains or just about anything else. Step-by-step instructions tell how it's done.

1. Quail pattern is enlarged on brown wrapping paper, then traced onto linoleum, which has been pre-sanded for better ink absorption. Colored areas, representing the finished, printed design, are filled in with a felt-tip pen.

2. Use a V-shaped gouge to cut the general outline of the design into the linoleum, almost to—but not through—the webbing on the back. Make a single cut around the more complex outlines. Cut should slope outward or the edge of the design will be undercut and weakened.

3. With a mat knife, cut into the middle of the outline trench, through webbing. Remove the background linoleum in one or two pieces and save.

4. Place background section of linoleum on a ¾″ plywood block. Outside edges of linoleum and wood

Exciting effects in this room are created with different pattern and color combinations of home-made prints for slipcovers, floor cushions, pillows, lampshades, bookcovers, curtains, tablecloths and a striking wall hanging. Printing process is described in text. Four motifs are used—two quail (one facing left, one right), a stylized chrysanthemum and a bumblebee. Patterns are shown for the quail and chrysanthemum; these are to be enlarged. The bumblebee is shown actual size and may be traced directly.

EACH SQUARE=1"

EACH SQUARE=1"

778

block should line up exactly. With a pencil, outline the design cutout. Place an even coating of water-resistant glue over the entire back surface (webbing side) of the cutout design. Place design on block and firmly press down all over.

5. Remove background linoleum and save again. Place glued block face-down on a wax paper-covered flat surface. Lay background section on back of block, webbing side up, and trace cutout design onto block with pencil or ink (this will serve as a guide when you are printing with the block). Remove background linoleum and weight the block evenly

with heavy books or bricks. Allow to set overnight.

6. The next day, cut away all uncolored areas of the design, using fine-tip cutting tools. Do not cut through webbing. With a damp cloth or paper towel, wipe the ink off the linoleum.

7. For extra security, hammer a few small finishing nails through the recessed areas of the linoleum into the plywood at key points.

8. When cutting is completed, test the linoleum design to make sure that all edges are clean cut. Pour a little ink onto a foil baking sheet or a piece of plate glass. Roll a brayer in

ink until evenly coated, then roll over design to coat evenly with color. Place a piece of tissue paper on a flat surface. Holding the block firmly at opposite edges, stamp the paper, making sure it doesn't shift and blur the print. Carefully raise the block. If any of the outlines are ragged, or if any ridges show where the larger areas have been cleared, correct the linoleum design. When you are satisfied with the design, wash the block over a bucket of water with a sponge, being careful not to soak the wood. Dry thoroughly with paper towels or a soft cloth.

9. Use paper cutouts to experiment with different arrangements before applying design to fabric. When you have decided, mark the outlines with chalk or pencil (light pencil lines can later be erased).

10. Choose water-soluble textile ink colors darker than the fabrics on which they are to be printed. Pour some ink onto the baking sheet or glass and roll out with a brayer until it is evenly coated. Roll the inked

brayer over the block design, coating it evenly. Try to prevent ink from accumulating in cut-away areas; if it does, wash off the block (see photos) and start over. Holding the inked block firmly at opposite edges, lower it onto the marked section of fabric.

11. Apply even pressure on the back of the block. Lean heavily on your hands.

12. Remove block from fabric with a single sure movement, raising it at an angle so that it can peel away from the fabric. Allow print to dry before adding more prints.

To set color permanently, wait un-

EACH SQUARE=1″

FABRIC

A: Remove background linoleum.

B: Cut design areas.

C: Nail down design.

D: Make a test run.

E: Figure the best layout.

G: Lean into it!

F: Press design on fabric.

H: Carefully lift block.

When using a linoleum cut to block-print designs on yardage, trace pattern onto linoleum, then cut general outline with V-shaped gouge, as described in text. Place design on a wood block (step 4 in text). Lay background linoleum on block and trace cutout, then remove linoleum (top left). Cut away appropriate areas of design (middle left, above), but do not cut through webbing on back of linoleum. Then, for extra security, hammer a few small finishing nails through the recessed areas of the linoleum into the plywood block at key points, as in middle right, above. Now it's time for a test run. Roll a brayer in ink until it is evenly coated, then coat the design evenly (top right). Hold the block firmly and stamp the design on a piece of tissue paper. Check the outline and the carved areas, and make any carving corrections necessary. Before printing on fabric, experiment by placing the tissue paper in different positions to determine the most pleasing arrangement (middle left). When you have decided on the best design, ink the brayer and evenly coat the block, then press it firmly onto the fabric (middle right). Once any part of the inked design touches the fabric, the whole block must follow with no sideways movement; otherwise you will get smears and double images. Apply even pressure on the back of the block, leaning on your hands as hard as you can (lower left). Remove the block from the fabric with one sure movement (lower right), raising it at an angle so that it peels away from the fabric. Allow print to dry before adding more prints, then repeat the procedure, inking the block again for each print.

Rich color tones highlight this room. The walls are covered with "Tulip Garden" fabric staple-gunned in place with a black-braid border to cover the staples. Window shades are made by simply ironing fabric onto a specially treated backing. Fabric on the upholstered Victorian sofa is quilted first to add dimension. The three types of pillows include a pair of prized needlepoint tulip designs, reversible velvet pillows with cutout flower appliques and plush floor pillows.

til ink has dried on fabric, then iron inked areas slowly and thoroughly (about 5 minutes) on the unprinted side of the fabric, with the iron dialed one setting lower than the appropriate temperature for the fabric. Do not use steam. Heat sets the color so that it remains "fast" through washing and dry cleaning.

Fans for Cooling

Fans built into the house are often used to ventilate the kitchen and bathroom or to cool the entire house. There are many types of fans available today. Some can be mounted in a window with two simple screws; they are removed for the winter.

In other cases, fans are mounted permanently. Kitchen exhaust fans are commonly used and are set through the wall.

Attic fans are used widely in many sections of the country. These fans can be mounted in the attic floor or in the attic wall. However, some handymen prefer to use a window-mounted fan, the installation of which is easier and quicker.

Basically, attic fans are nothing more than ventilating fans which have been used for years in restaurant kitchens, modified of course, for quieter operation and greater capacity. The average size is from 30″ to 36″ in diameter. Large sizes are made, but are needed only for very large homes. The number of blades varies from 3 to 6 with a pitch of 30° to 40°. This permits the fan to move a large amount of air while turning at a fairly low speed, which is essential to quiet operation. Fans smaller than 30″ are usually considered window fans, not because they are too small for use in attics but because they are about as large as can be mounted in the average window.

With an attic fan, you simply turn it on about sundown and it pulls out the hot air that fills the house, and permits the cooler outside air to take its place. This not only lowers the air temperature, but the cooler air actually absorbs the stored up heat in the walls and ceiling of the house. In the average house, the air is changed every two or three minutes. This rapid change is essential for good cooling, since the temperature differential is only a few degrees, and the greatest possible differential is essential to the rapid transfer of heat.

With a window fan, this warmed air is discharged directly outdoors, preferably on the side of the house away from the prevailing wind.

An attic fan discharges the slightly warmed air into the intensely hot interior of the attic, where daytime temperatures may reach 130° or more, forcing out this hot air and cooling the structural members of the house before escaping through the openings provided, which may be windows or louvers, or both. Since these openings should be screened against insects, the combined area should be at least 50% greater than the area of the fan—around 7½ square feet for a 30″ fan, or about 12 square feet for a 36″ fan.

It is preferable that the fan exhaust away from the principal outlet, to secure the maximum of tur-

782

bulence, so there will be no isolated pockets of hot air to retard the cooling of the attic. This procedure assures that the house will be adequately cooled even by the children's bedtime.

If your situation is such that you cannot make an attic installation, a window fan will give you most of the benefits. You probably won't be able to turn it off at bedtime, as you usually can do with the attic fan, but even if it has to run all night, the cost will be low.

Attic Ventilation

In homes with open attics, which are floored, the fan may discharge through a window or through an opening provided for ventilation, either in an end wall or in a dormer placed in the sloping part of the roof. In both cases the air is discharged directly to the outside, the attic acting as a plenum chamber. This fan installation should be protected from the weather by either louvers or a rain hood.

For the houses with flat roofs, it is necessary to construct a penthouse or cupola which is connected directly to the finished ceiling opening by an air shaft.

LOCATION OF VENTILATING UNIT—The fans which must exhaust directly to the outside must be located so that they discharge with, and not against, the prevailing wind in your location.

Fans which exhaust into the attic from the space below should be located as centrally as possible from all the rooms to be ventilated. The discharge from the fan must be as far as possible from adjacent walls, chimneys, etc.

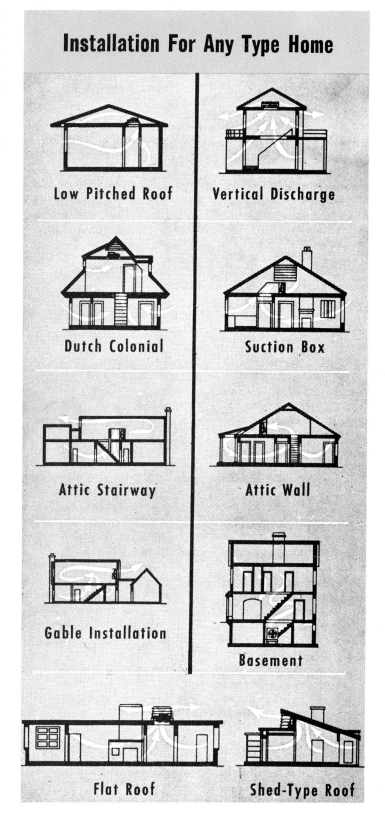

Installation For Any Type Home

Low Pitched Roof

Vertical Discharge

Dutch Colonial

Suction Box

Attic Stairway

Attic Wall

Gable Installation

Basement

Flat Roof

Shed-Type Roof

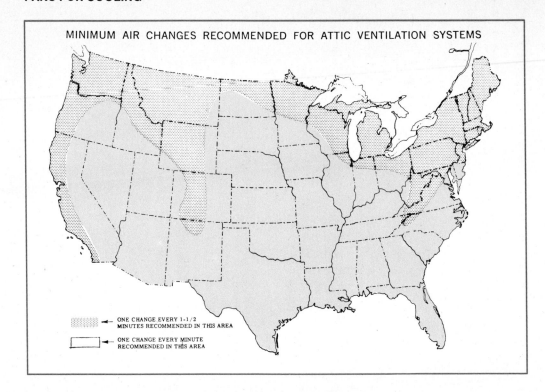

MINIMUM AIR CHANGES RECOMMENDED FOR ATTIC VENTILATION SYSTEMS

ONE CHANGE EVERY 1-1/2 MINUTES RECOMMENDED IN THIS AREA

ONE CHANGE EVERY MINUTE RECOMMENDED IN THIS AREA

784

FAN UNIT CHARACTERIS-TICS—Quiet operation is the most desirable fan unit characteristic. It can be belt or direct-connected, be mounted in a substantial frame and be equipped with a resilient mounted motor or some form of shock and sound absorbing characteristic. The resistance against which the fan must operate is determined by the size of the air intakes and exhaust openings (louvers). If openings smaller than the recommended sizes are used, the resistance increases and the volume of air handled by the fan is reduced.

AIR CHANGES PER MINUTE —A definite figure cannot be set up for the number of air changes per minute. The rate of air change depends not only on the climate and locality but upon the individual preference. Practice and past experience have determined that in

95% of the cases in the South a net air change of once a minute is satisfactory. For locations in parts of the North it is satisfactory and comfortable to change the air once every minute and a half.

FAN SELECTION—It is necessary to determine the cubic content of your house in order to select the right size fan to cool it. Only an approximate figure is needed; just multiply the width and depth of your home by the height. This will give you the approximate number of cubic feet in your home.

If you live in the Southern part of the United States (see *MAP SHOWING AIR CHANGES*), you will need a fan capable of changing the required number of feet every minute.

If you live in the northern section where an air change is needed every 1½ minutes, take two-thirds of the cubic content of your home. Buy a fan that will displace that cubic volume every minute.

It is better to buy a fan that will displace or move a somewhat greater amount than the actual cubic content of your home calls for. In this way, there will be less of a strain on the fan and you'll find yourself more comfortable on those especially hot and humid days.

AIR VELOCITIES THROUGH INLET GRILLE AND FAN UNIT—The air velocities through the ceiling grilles must not exceed 750 feet per minute, to keep air noise and static pressure as low as possible. The average velocity of the air leaving the fan ranges from 1200 to 1400 feet per minute. With this knowledge we can establish a rough ratio for ceiling grille area to fan orifice area at approximately two to one. This ratio is based on a net grille opening of 84% of the gross area.

ATTIC DISCHARGE VENTS (LOUVERS)—Correct area and location are the most important factors to be considered. There should always be a number of discharge vents rather than just one. A head wind from any single direction has little effect on the performance of the fan, if a number of openings are employed at different points of the compass.

All discharge vents must be covered with ½″ hardware cloth to keep out birds.

INSTALLATION OF VARIOUS FAN TYPES—There are two types of fans, (1) fans which discharge horizontally; (2) fans which discharge vertically.

(1) Horizontal discharge fans are usually installed in an outside wall if the attic is finished, on the attic floor with a plenum chamber if the attic is unfinished, or in a penthouse or cupola if the building has a flat roof. A fan mounted in an outside wall or in a penthouse requires a tailor-made installation to meet the special conditions.

A fan installed in a prefabricated

Typical Discharge Openings

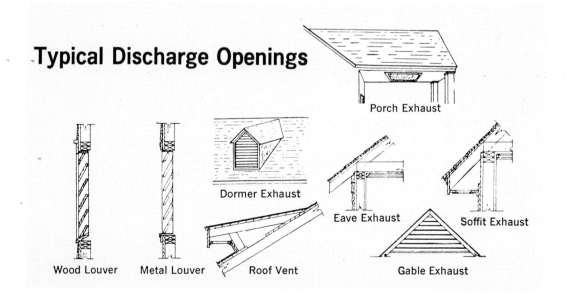

Porch Exhaust

Dormer Exhaust

Eave Exhaust

Soffit Exhaust

Wood Louver

Metal Louver

Roof Vent

Gable Exhaust

MINIMUM GROSS OUTLET AREAS FOR ATTIC FAN DISCHARGE VENTS

Areas	1 Minute Air Change	1½ Minute Air Change
Wood louvers backed with ½" hardware cloth.	Not less than 1/40 of the gross floor area.	Not less than 1/60 of the gross floor area.
Metal louvers backed with ½" hardware cloth.	Not less than 1/50 of the gross floor area.	Not less than 1/90 of the gross floor area.
Other openings such as those in soffits, etc. Plain openings backed with ½" hardware cloth.	Not less than 1/65 of the gross floor area.	Not less than 1/100 of the gross floor area.

If louvers or openings are covered with No. 16 mesh screen, add a minimum of 100% of the gross louver area. This may be done by:
 a. Doubling the size of the louver or opening.
 b. Constructing a box-like frame behind the louver or opening with a screened surface twice the area of the louver.

plenum chamber usually meets the requirements of the installation. Prefabricated plenum chambers are constructed of sound-deadening material supported on a skeleton wooden frame. The top of the plenum chamber may be horizontal or it may slope down from the fan.

In an automatic shutter installation, the vanes should open towards the fan in the same direction as the air flow. The shutters should cover the entire suction opening and be of such size as not to restrict the air flow.

The fan case must be mounted on rubber pads, springs, or on a sound deadening pad. The fan and plenum chamber installation consists of mounting the unit on a platform extending over the grille. The plenum chamber must be as nearly airtight as possible to get the utmost benefit of fan capacity in the area being ventilated rather than merely re-circulating the air.

(2) Vertical discharge fans are installed in the attic floor of unfinished attics or in the penthouse or cupola in buildings which have a flat roof. The plenum chamber is not necessary because the fan is mounted directly over the ceiling opening. A sound-isolating padding or other material must be placed between the fan and the supporting frame. Automatic or hand operated shutters are required below the fan to close the ceiling opening when the fan is not operating.

PROTECTION AGAINST WINTER HEAT LOSS—In the winter the openings, whether louvers, porch grilles, soffit outlets or others should have removable covers of insulation board. A similar cover should be provided for the grille opening or automatic shutter.

ELECTRICAL INSTALLATION—A separate circuit from the main service entrance panel should be provided to feed attic fan installations using motors of 1/3 H.P. and better. A fused disconnect switch in the hall or other easily accessible location must be provided. In the event of fire, an automatic method must be provided for cutting off the fan and closing the ceiling opening. A fusible link, set to open at 135° F. is recommended for this purpose and is installed in the air stream. It is placed on the suction side of the fan to operate a cut-off switch in series with the fan.

Where the installation includes a trap door, the fuse releases it and closes the ceiling opening. In the automatic shutter installation, they are closed when the fan stops. The fan motors can be provided with automatic thermal cut-outs to prevent overheating of the motor. This precaution will prevent the motor from becoming a fire hazard as well as preventing the motor from burning out due to any overload.

OPERATING HINTS AND SUGGESTIONS—Check all bearings for lubrication. Oil the motor and fan bearings according to the manufacturer's directions.

Examine the belt for tension and alignment.

The fan will pull soot and dirt down the chimney if there is no other way for air to enter, so be sure to open a window before starting the fan.

During the initial operation of the fan check for noise sources, loose parts, and for loose floor boards on the attic joists.

After the fan has been operating for a few weeks examine the fan belt for tension. Make any necessary adjustments in accordance with the manufacturers instructions.

Make a note on your calendar to thoroughly examine and oil the fan every year.

An attic fan mounted in the floor of the attic will draw the hot air out of the rooms in the house letting cool, fresh air come in through the windows.

An attic fan is mounted to fit into an opening cut in the joists. Here the fan is mounted horizontally, but with a special box chamber, it can be mounted vertically in the chamber or even in an exterior wall in the roof.

788

Sketches courtesy of Propeller Fan Manufacturer's Association.

The opening in the ceiling is covered by a special louver grille. This protects fingers and other objects from getting in the way of the fan blades and also keeps the attic sealed closed when the fan is not in operation.

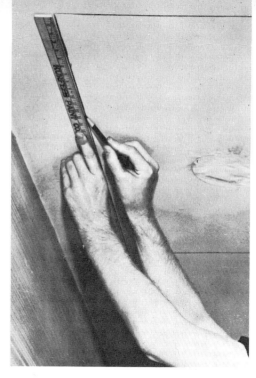

1. Locate the position of one of the ceiling joists and then mark the area to be covered by the fan. Try to cut as few ceiling joists as possible. This is done to reduce the amount of work; cutting even three joists (and this is not necessary with a home fan) usually will not affect the structure of the house. Actually, you will probably have to cut only a single joist, two at the most.

How to Install an Attic Fan

After deciding upon the best size fan for your home, make certain that there is space for the unit in a convenient place where the fan will be able to draw air from all the rooms in about equal amounts. If the fan is located at one end of the house, it is likely to cool the rooms

3. If you have a dry-wall material for a ceiling, you can use a portable electric or hand saw to do the cutting job. If you do not have the power tools, it is best to drill a 1″ diameter hole at each corner and then remove the inside section by cutting with a keyhole or compass saw.

Photographs courtesy of Robbins & Myers, Inc.

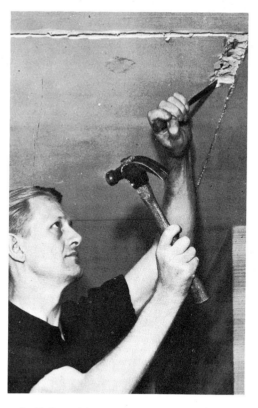

2. If the ceiling is made of plaster, score along the drawn line with a sharp cold chisel and then chop out the plaster, using a cold chisel and a hammer. Remember, do not try to chop the plaster out until you have made the score marks; otherwise, you may crack the ceiling outside the area to be removed for the fan.

789

4. Remove the rest of the ceiling covering material and expose the joists overhead. Cut the joists with a crosscut saw or a portable electric saw as close to the outside edges of the opening as possible.

5. Use the cut pieces of the joists or wood of same thickness and width to join the cut edges of the joists on each side of the opening. Generally, you can use the cut pieces because the opening for most attic fans is cut in the shape of a square.

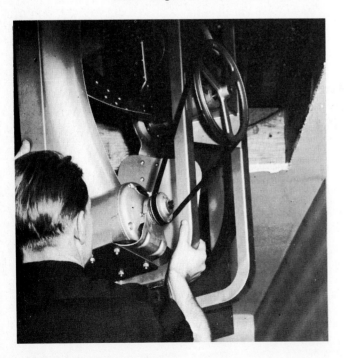

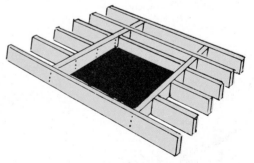

6. Get a helper to assist you and lift the entire fan unit into the attic through the cut opening. You will have to keep the fan at an angle so that it goes through easily.

Photographs courtesy of Robbins & Myers, Inc.

7. Check the opening nailed for the fan to see that it is the same size as the base of the fan unit. If it is, have your helper assist you in setting the fan assembly over the opening. It is best to glue some rubber cushioning material along the top edge of the opening, if such a cushion is not provided as part of fan mounting.

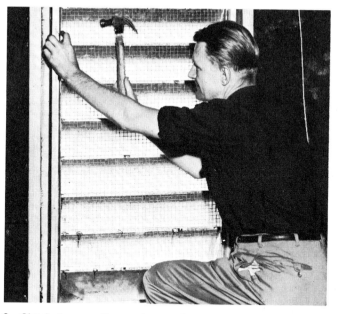

8. Install the louver grille opening below. This comes in one piece, usually of metal, and is set in place with screws. If you use long screws, you will be able to drive them through the ceiling material into the joists overhead. Connect the fan motor wire to an outlet which is wired to a switch downstairs in the hallway or wherever the fan is located.

9. Check to see if you have adequate openings in the attic for the fan to operate properly. See the accompanying copy and table showing the size of openings needed. If the opening is too small, the fan will not operate at its maximum efficiency—there will be no place in the attic for it to force the air out of. Cover the opening to keep insects out.

nearer to it rather than the rooms at the other end of the house.

Installing an attic fan is a simple job, but having a helper makes the work easier; it also speeds the job. Here in photograph form is the step-by-step technique.

All you need in the way of tools —stepladder, ruler, compass saw, crosscut saw, brace and bits or portable electric drill, cold chisel, wood chisel, screwdriver and hammer, plus the tools for adding a new outlet and a switch to control the fan. A portable electric saw will be very useful, if available.

Fascia

A broad band used in combination with moldings. Generally, this term is used to describe the special wood trim covering the joint between the exterior walls of the house and roof.

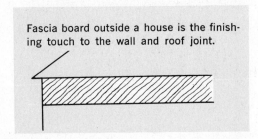

Fascia board outside a house is the finishing touch to the wall and roof joint.

Faucets

Faucets generally used in homes are of three types: compression, Fuller ball, and ground-key.

The compression type of faucet is usually fitted with a lever or four-ball handle which offers firm resistance to efforts to turn down the spindle much beyond the point where the flow of water stops. The stem of the spindle may be seen to move in or out of the body of the faucet when the handle is turned. A self-closing faucet is usually of the compression type.

Fuller ball faucets are generally fitted with a lever handle and the stem does not move in or out of the body of the faucet when the handle is turned. When a Fuller ball is in good condition, the handle should require but one-quarter turn to open or close the flow opening.

The ground-key faucet is easily distinguished by the lever handle and plunger, which is made in one piece, and by the exposed nut or screw at the lower end which holds the plunger in place.

It is sometimes impossible to determine the type of faucet from the outside appearance. If so, the only way to find out will be to dismantle it. At the same time, the kind and size of washer or Fuller ball may be determined and the condition of the brass screw examined to see whether or not it needs replacing.

Compression

In the ordinary compression-type faucet the flow of water is regu-

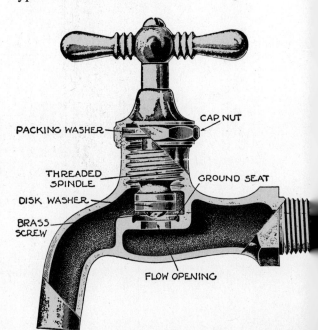

PACKING WASHER

CAP NUT

THREADED SPINDLE

GROUND SEAT

DISK WASHER

BRASS SCREW

FLOW OPENING

Don't let a dripping faucet drive you to distraction— it's a problem that is easily cured.

lated by turning a lever, T, or four-ball handle which is attached to a threaded spindle. When the spindle is turned down, the washer or disk attached to its lower end is pressed tightly against the smoothly finished ring or ground seat which surrounds the flow opening, thus shutting off the flow of water. If the washer and the seat do not make a firm contact at all points, water will leak through and drip from the faucet. A leak usually results from a wornout washer. If washers wear out rapidly, it may be because a poor grade of washer is being used, because the ground seat has become sharp and rough as a result of corrosion, or because the seat has become scratched or worn by grit.

Moderate force on the handle of a compression-type faucet in good repair should stop all flow and drip. If a leak develops, it may be caused by faulty washers which are not difficult to replace. It is important that faucets be tightly closed after they are used because dripping faucets tend to produce or aggravate leaks, waste water, and result in rust stains on porcelain surfaces. Soon after a hot-water faucet has been shut off and the water cools, contraction takes place which may cause a drip to develop. Should this occur, the spigot handle should be tightened without opening while the faucet is still cool.

The following tools and materials are needed: Wrench, screwdriver, fiber or special composition washers for compression-type faucets.

To avoid frequent renewals, a good grade of washer should be selected. The sizes most frequently

793

used are ⅜″, ½″ and ⅝″ and it is well to have a supply of each size on hand. Composition washers sometimes have one side flat and the other side slightly rounded. A good contact is made with this type of washer because, by fitting partly down into the seat of the faucet, it is subject to both horizontal and vertical pressure. Some faucets require specially shaped washers, the size and type of which should be determined for replacement.

To renew a washer, shut off the water directly below the fixture or in the main water supply pipe. If the water is shut off by the valve in the main pipe and there are fixtures located higher than the one in which the washers are to be replaced, the riser pipes to the higher fixtures should be drained before disassembling the faucet. If this is not done, it may be impossible to control the

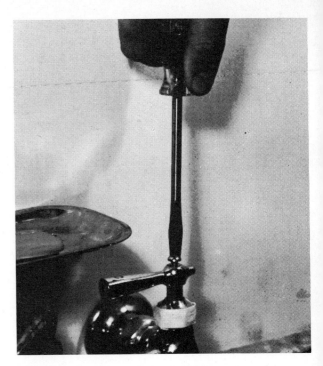

2. Take off the handle by removing the screw that holds it to the top of the spindle. There may be a knurled nut or snap-on button over the screw head which must be removed first.

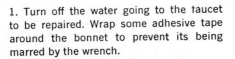

1. Turn off the water going to the faucet to be repaired. Wrap some adhesive tape around the bonnet to prevent its being marred by the wrench.

3. Remove the bonnet by turning counterclockwise with a wrench. The adhesive tape will protect the finish.

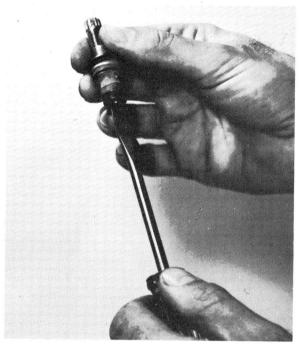

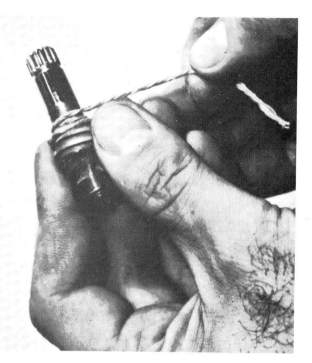

4. Slip spindle out of bonnet and remove washer by taking out the screw that holds it. Replace it with a washer of identical size made of fiber, rubber or plastic.

6. Slip bonnet over spindle and check packing. If worn, replace it by twisting on impregnated cord which you can buy at a local hardware store. Wind in clockwise direction from bottom to top.

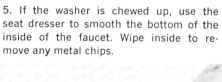

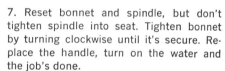

5. If the washer is chewed up, use the seat dresser to smooth the bottom of the inside of the faucet. Wipe inside to remove any metal chips.

7. Reset bonnet and spindle, but don't tighten spindle into seat. Tighten bonnet by turning clockwise until it's secure. Replace the handle, turn on the water and the job's done.

flow of water issuing from the faucet when taken apart. If shut-offs located directly below the fixtures are used, this precaution will not be necessary. Then, with a wrench (using a cloth to protect the fixture from being marred), unscrew the cap nut of the faucet to allow the spindle to be unscrewed and removed. Carefully remove the brass screw that holds the washer to the bottom of the spindle, and replace the worn washer with a new one. If the head of the brass screw is badly worn, it will be difficult to remove and may be twisted off, unless handled carefully. A drop or two of kerosene and gently tapping the screw may help to loosen it in the stem. The screwdriver should have a good square edge and should be turned with a strong steady pressure. If the head of the screw chips off or breaks so that it does not hold the screwdriver, the slot will have to be deepened, if possible by cutting into the head with a hack saw. A badly worn screw should always be replaced.

A worn or roughened washer seat can often be ground true and smooth with a faucet seat-dressing tool. Such a tool is inexpensive and will probably more than pay for itself within a reasonable time. One type consists of a stem with a cutter at the lower end and a wheel handle at the top to rotate the tool. It is fitted with a spiraled cone to be inserted into the body of the faucet and screwed down firmly for the purpose of centering and holding the cutter on the washer seat. When the tool is properly placed, it should be carefully rotated back and forth several times with the wheel handle until the seat is ground free of irregularities. When the grinding is finished, all metal cuttings should be wiped out with a cloth before the faucet is reassembled. If the seat is in such bad condition that it does not respond to this treatment and continues to cut the washers, it will be necessary to substitute a new faucet.

If water leaks around the stem when the faucet is open, it may frequently be stopped by tightening the cap nut, but the nut should not be made so tight as to cause the faucet to bind. If tightening does not stop the leak, it is probable that the packing washers under the cap nut are worn out and need renewing. To put in new washers, remove the handle and cap nut and substitute new washers for the old. To stop the leakage temporarily, wrap a small piece of oil-soaked candle-wicking or soft string around the stem, under the cap nut where the stem enters the body of the faucet.

Fuller Ball

In the Fuller ball faucet, a hard rubber or composition ball-like stopper, known as the Fuller ball, is fastened by a small nut or screw to a shaft with an eccentric end. When the faucet handle is closed, this ball is drawn firmly against the opening, shutting off the flow of water; when the handle is opened, the ball is pushed away from the opening, allowing the water to pass through. The best grade of Fuller ball should be used; the sizes range from 3/8" to 1".

To replace a Fuller ball, the water should be shut off and the faucet unscrewed and separated from the supply pipe. The nut or screw should be taken off with pliers or a screwdriver and the ball removed and replaced with a new one.

Sometimes the metal axle which holds the Fuller ball or the eccentric part becomes worn, making it impossible to pull the ball tight against the seat, and allowing leakage between the ball and the seat. If this happens, it will be necessary to purchase new metal parts to replace the worn ones. If water leaks out around the stem when the faucet is open, repairs can be made in the same manner as prescribed for similar leakage in compression-type faucets.

Ground-Key

The ground-key faucet has a tapered cylindrical brass plunger or plug which should fit snugly into a sleeve, bored vertically through the body of the faucet. The plunger, which is rotated by a handle, has a hole or slot bored horizontally through it, to coincide with a similarly shaped horizontal opening in the body of the faucet. When the handle that rotates the plunger is parallel to the body of the faucet, the two openings are in line with each other and allow the water to pass through. A short turn of the

Ground-key faucet.

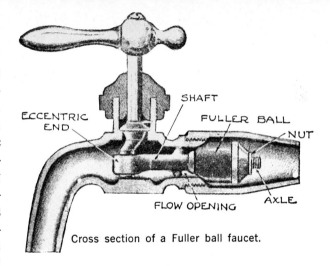

Cross section of a Fuller ball faucet.

handle to the right or left throws the opening out of line and cuts off the flow.

The plunger or its sleeve may become grooved or worn by sand particles rubbing against the metal and allow the water to leak through. This requires repolishing of the rubbing surfaces. Also, the nut or screw at the bottom may become loose, permitting the plunger to move out of its proper position, allowing leakage. On the other hand, if the nut or screw is too tight, the plunger will bind and will be difficult to turn.

Noise in Faucets

Sometimes when a faucet is partly turned on or suddenly closed, a water hammer, tapping, or pounding noise is heard. In a compression-type faucet, this may be caused by a loose cap nut, a worn spindle, or a defective washer. In a Fuller ball faucet, the ball may become loose, or the metal eccentric connecting the handle to the Fuller ball may become worn.

The following tools are needed: wrench, screwdriver, and pliers.

To eliminate noise in a compression-type faucet, shut off the water and remove the spindle and washer so that they may be ex-

797

amined. If the washer is found to be loose, the brass screw should be tightened; if the washer is worn, the brass screw should be removed and a new washer attached. If the threads on the spindle or in the body of the faucet are badly worn, letting the spindle rattle, it will be necessary to purchase a new faucet.

If the faucet is of the Fuller ball type, shut off the water and tighten the small nut or screw which holds the Fuller ball; if the ball is badly worn it should be replaced. If parts

of the eccentric are worn and tend to rattle, the faucet should be taken to a plumber. If the eccentric is beyond repair and new parts cannot be obtained, it will be necessary to install a new faucet.

Outside Faucet

Having running water available outside your home is a great convenience. It's simple to attach a garden hose for watering the lawn or shrubs or washing the car.

Here's what you have to do to add a faucet for outside your home:

1. Decide upon the location of the faucet and make an opening for the pipe in the outside wall of your home.

2. If you have to go through a concrete block foundation wall, use a masonry bit with an electric drill or a star drill and hammer.

3. If you go through the wooden section of your house, use an expansion bit with a brace to make the opening through the wall for the pipe to pass through.

4. Find the nearest convenient place to join this outside water pipe to the house line.

5. Shut off the main water or the branch line to be cut. It is best if you can avoid breaking into a line; if it is at all possible to hook in at a fitting, do so.

6. Insert a T-fitting in the line and connect pipe to the hole in the wall. See *PLUMBING* for the how-to.

7. A drainable valve should be used inside the house to control the flow of water to the line. This valve has a special cap or screw opening to permit draining the water out of the line (between this valve and the outside hose cock), so that no water

798

FAUCET PARTS

- Handle Screw
- Handle
- Cap Nut (a)
- Cone Bonnet Packing (b)
- Top Bibb Washer
- Stem
- Faucet Washer (c)
- Bibb Screw (d)
- Cone Slip Joint Washer
- Brass Friction Ring

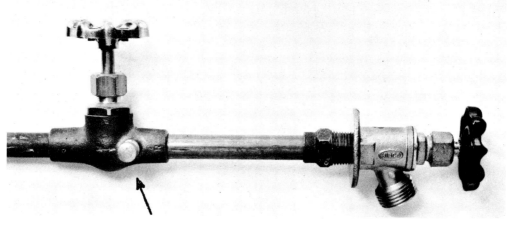

Hose cock installation showing the placement of the drainable valve on the inside of the house.

freezes during the cold weather and bursts the pipe.

8. Install the drainable valve so that the drain cap or screw is on the side toward the hose cock.

9. Attach a piece of pipe to this valve and through the wall.

10. A hose cock is attached on the other side of the wall. To keep the pipe steady, force a few wooden wedges between the pipe and the exterior wall and then calk the opening.

11. Now the main water valve or branch water line valve can be opened and the outside faucet is ready to use.

In the winter, when the outside faucet is not in use, shut off the drainable valve and then open the outside hose cock. After the water has dripped out of the pipe, open the drain cap or screw to let the remaining water trickle out. Keep this cap off and the hose cock open for the winter months.

If it is necessary to use water during exceedingly cold weather, you can obtain a hydrant-type valve. This is a special valve where the seat or base is about 24″ or more

away from the handle. Thus, when the water is shut off, there is little danger of it freezing and expanding to burst the pipe. Note that when installing this type of a valve, it should be pitched downward to permit proper drainage.

Normally, a compression type of faucet is used to control the flow of water outside the house. A hose cock is merely a special type of compression faucet with its end threaded to receive a hose coupling. However, if you live in an area with low water pressure, you should use a gate valve with a hose coupling adapter. The gate valve does not constrict the flow of water nor does it reduce the water pressure.

799

Fences and Gates

There are as many types of fences and gates as there are houses. The fence should be built to conform to the style of the house and the size of the ground which it bounds, and it should be sturdy so that it fulfills its functional as well as decorative value.

Wood Fences

The rails may be bought ready-cut at a lumber yard. Or you may prefer to cut them yourself. Get the best quality wood you can afford as the fence must stand a long time; the wood needs to retain the paint, and you want to avoid replacement if possible. A durable, close-grained wood, therefore, is recommended.

Gate and Fence Posts

Special care must be given to the wood used for the posts, as they must be sturdy. The post ends, which go into the ground, should be treated with a modern wood preservative such as Woodlife, or creosote which is heated to about 200° F. may be brushed on to the wood ends. This acts as a decay preventative. The wood must be thoroughly dry and no pieces of bark must adhere to the posts. (Caution: creosote, if used, is flammable, so proceed with care when heating it!)

Fence Construction

It is impossible to go into the details of all types, as they range from the traditional picket fence to the modern ranch-style. Generally, however, the way to proceed is to measure off the distances at which the posts will be spaced. Then mark each post at the point where the horizontal top and bottom cross-rails will go. Cut out the notches on the posts for these cross-rails. Mark, measure, and cut the upright fence

800

rails. If the fence is to be placed on ground which is not level, some of the posts and upright rails may need to be cut shorter or longer to accommodate uneven ground level.

Now dig out the holes for the posts. Set the first post in the ground, and pour in concrete or tamp the earth around it. (Concrete has the advantage of holding posts very firmly and is, of course, essential for iron fence supports. However, posts of any durable wood, if treated with a modern wood preservative, will last a long time in well-drained earth. In many cases, therefore, it is optional with the handyman which method he selects.) Follow the same method with the second post. Then nail the two horizontal rails across the two posts; or, if you do not use nails, insert the cross-rails into cut-out holes or notches (depending on the style you have chosen for your fence). Continue this process of setting posts and nailing or inserting cross-rails until they are all in place, and open space is left for the gate (if a gate is to be included).

Your next step is to nail the upright rails to the top and bottom cross-rails. You may prefer to nail the uprights as you work along; for instance between the first and second post; then when that is done, the cross-rails and the uprights between the second and third post. The rails may be spaced as far apart as you desire.

The nails and other hardware you use should, of course, be rust-proof and weatherproof.

You may want to leave the wood fence unpainted. However, if you paint it, be sure to use exterior paint.

Reinforced fiberglas panels lend themselves to use in fences with results which are both practical as well as attractive. The material is durable and requires little or no maintenance and is easily worked. Shown here are some fence ideas as modern as the material.

Photos courtesy Filon Corporation

801

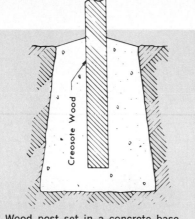

Wood post set in a concrete base.

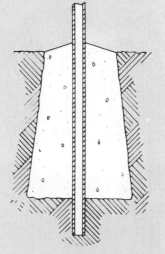

Pipe or metal post set in concrete.

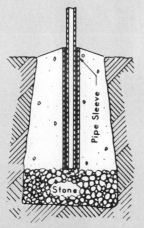

A wood pole (1" or larger dowel) set in a metal sleeve in concrete. The pole can be removed while the sleeve remains imbedded in the concrete.

Sketches courtesy of Sakrete, Inc.

Gate Hanging

You may find a ready-made gate at the lumber yard which fits the size and style of the fence. Otherwise, you could make your own gate, first building a framework, then proceeding with the rails to follow the general pattern of the fence. The gate is hung on the post with hinges which are durable and rustproof. A latch is attached to the opposite side of the gate and its adjacent post. The gate is then painted or left in its natural state, to correspond with the fence.

Brick Fence

This, of course, is not usually considered as informal as the wood fence. However, a brick fence is a solid wall for shrubs and vines if you want them for your garden. The color and design of the brick wall is a personal choice. The bricks are laid with mortar, as discussed in the section on *BRICK*.

A wood gate is appropriate with a brick fence. The gate may follow the general style of the house ifself, and then be painted either the color of the brick or a dominant color used on the house exterior.

How to Set Fence Posts

To set wood or concrete posts, dig a hole from 1½' to 3' deep, depending upon the height of the post. The hole should be about 8" to 12" square at the top.

For best results, make the bottom of the hole somewhat wider than the top so as to resist any tipping effect on the post. Then pour about 4" of concrete (ready-mixed saves you time if a large number of posts have to be set) into the bottom of the hole. Set the post into position and hold it securely by attaching a few 1x4 or 2x4 braces to it. Then pour concrete to fill the remainder of the hole, making certain to tamp the mixture down as you pour.

It is good policy to apply a coat of wood preservative over the base of the post before it is submerged in the concrete. A coating of asphalt is sometimes substituted.

If you use a metal post, it is not necessary to dig the hole as wide as for a wood post. In setting the metal post, however, it is advisable to sink the post about 6″ below the bottom of the hole before pouring in the concrete.

Always finish the top of the concrete off so that the water flows away from the post. A trowel is used for this job.

Planning a Picket Fence

Certain basic dimensions should be followed when making a picket fence. It has been found over the years that certain proportions and certain placement of parts produce the most pleasing effects. Here is a guide for building.

• Post should be made of 4x4 lumber and should extend about 36″ above the ground. Two feet should extend below ground level.

• The posts should be no more than 8′ apart unless you plan to use stringers of lumber heavier than 2x4's.

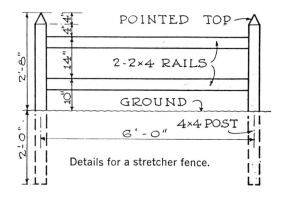

Details for a stretcher fence.

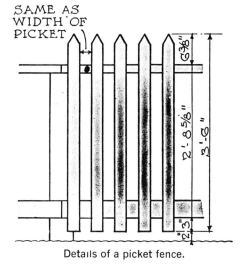

Details of a picket fence.

Patterns for picket tops.

803

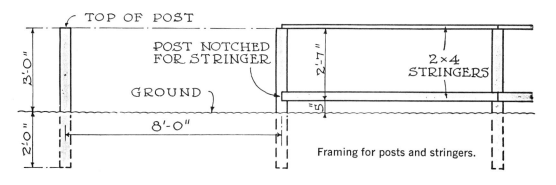

Framing for posts and stringers.

Simple board-and-batten fence insures privacy for this small off-bedroom patio.

- The bottom stringer should be about 5" above the ground level.
- When the pickets are mounted, the bottom edge should be about 2" above the ground level.
- The pickets should be about 42" long and extend about 6" above the top stringer and 3" below the bottom stringer.
- The space between the pickets should be the same as the width of the individual pickets.

Ready-Made Fences

Many homeowners would rather not spend the time needed to make their own fence. They prefer buying ready-made fences and installing them around their property. Frequently, buying a ready-made fence is not more expensive than making your own. Before you build, if you plan a conventional fence, it pays to shop around. If there is not too much price differential and you prefer to spend your time doing other jobs, you might want a ready-made fence.

804

Conventional post and rail fence adds a distinctive touch to any property. It is easy to construct out of rough-cut logs or the parts can be purchased and set up on your property.

This attractive fence is made of heavy, prewoven hardwood veneer. The basket weave pattern combines smart ornamentation with privacy and with safety for small children and pets.

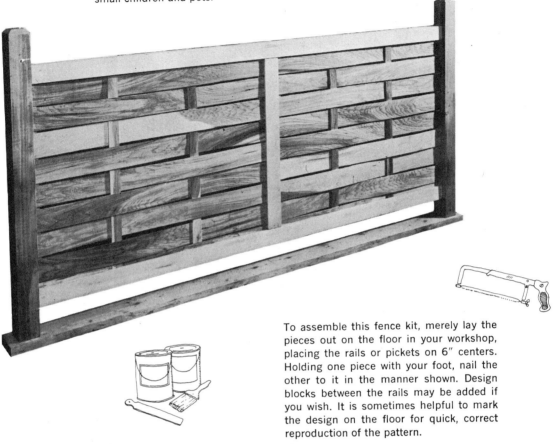

To assemble this fence kit, merely lay the pieces out on the floor in your workshop, placing the rails or pickets on 6″ centers. Holding one piece with your foot, nail the other to it in the manner shown. Design blocks between the rails may be added if you wish. It is sometimes helpful to mark the design on the floor for quick, correct reproduction of the pattern.

805

Distinctive Fences of Hardboard

Inexpensive tempered hardboard can be used to make unusual fences. Here are three patterns which you can easily make for your home by following simple fence construction techniques.

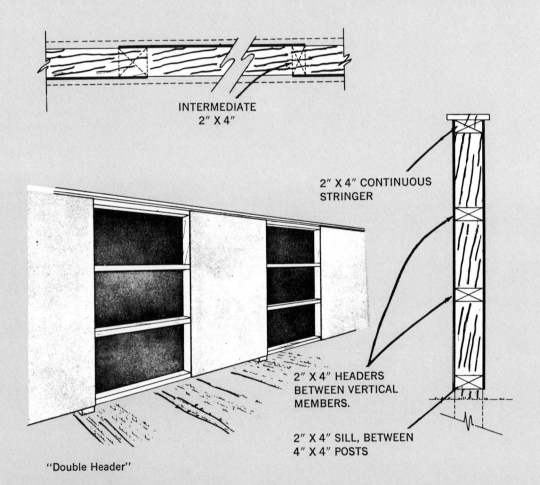

INTERMEDIATE
2" X 4"

2" X 4" CONTINUOUS
STRINGER

2" X 4" HEADERS
BETWEEN VERTICAL
MEMBERS.

2" X 4" SILL, BETWEEN
4" X 4" POSTS

"Double Header"

806

Sketch courtesy of Masonite Corp.

DOUBLE HEADER—This fence with 4x4 posts and 2x4's as stringers is covered with sheets of tempered hardboard. Note that the sheets are overlapped in a shadow wall effect. One sheet is nailed in place on one side of the stringers and the next sheet is set on the opposite side.

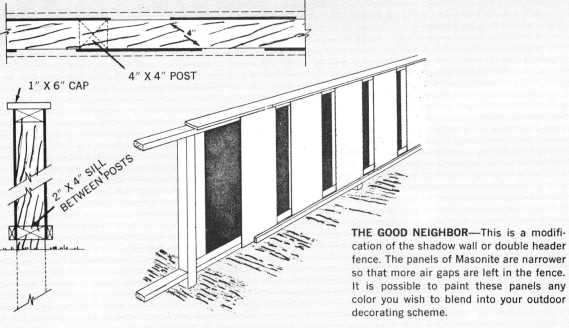

1" X 6" CAP

4" X 4" POST

2" X 4" SILL BETWEEN POSTS

THE GOOD NEIGHBOR—This is a modification of the shadow wall or double header fence. The panels of Masonite are narrower so that more air gaps are left in the fence. It is possible to paint these panels any color you wish to blend into your outdoor decorating scheme.

Sketch courtesy of Masonite Corp.

HANGING GARDEN—Using perforated hardboard outdoors will produce an exciting new type of fence. A sheet of perforated board is set in as part of any contemporary fence. The shelf brackets and adaptors are used to support flowering plants.

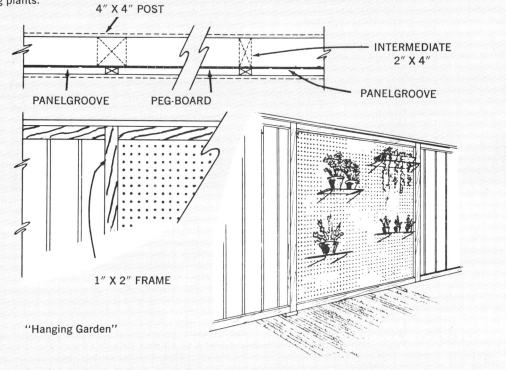

4" X 4" POST

INTERMEDIATE 2" X 4"

PANELGROOVE   PEG-BOARD

PANELGROOVE

1" X 2" FRAME

"Hanging Garden"

807

Contemporary Fences with Reinforced Plastic Panels

You can give your home a new look, brighten up your lawn and garden and insure 'no trespassing' with a fence made with reinforced plastic panels. These panels are translucent and shatterproof and can be sawed, nailed and drilled—just like wood. They are available in many different colors in flat or corrugated form.

These fences are incredibly strong, dentproof and rotproof. You admit the light with the translucent panels but maintain privacy.

SCREENING FENCE—If you want complete privacy, here's the fence for you. With this tall screen-fence, you can close off your outdoor living area from your neighbor's view or hide unsightly burners, compost heaps and unattractive views.

Sketches courtesy of Monsanto Chemical Co.

808

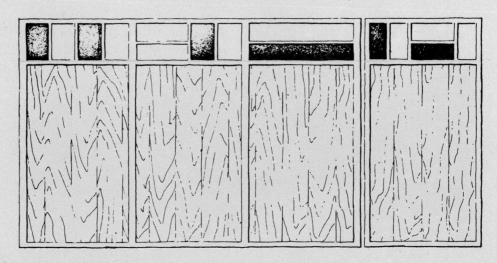

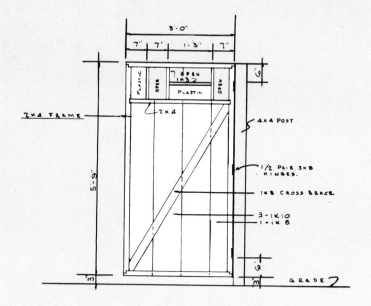

3'-0"

7" 7" 1'-3" 7"

PLASTIC OPEN OPEN 1X2 OPEN

PLASTIC

2X4

2X4 FRAME

4X4 POST

1/2 PAIR 3X8 HINGES.

1X8 CROSS BRACE

3-1X10
1-1X 8

5'-9"

3"

3"

6

6

GRADE

3"

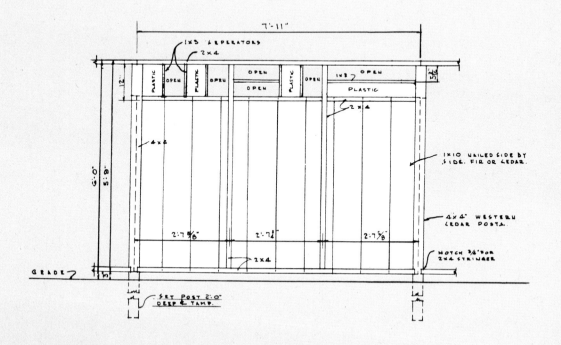

7'-11"

1X3 SEPERATORS

2X4

PLASTIC OPEN PLASTIC OPEN OPEN PLASTIC OPEN 1X2 OPEN

OPEN

PLASTIC

2X4

12"

5½"

4X4

1X10 NAILED SIDE BY SIDE. FIR OR CEDAR.

6'-0"

5'-9"

2'-7⅝" 2'-7¼" 2'-7⅝"

2X4

4X4" WESTERN CEDAR POSTS.

NOTCH ¾"FOR 2X4 STRINGER

GRADE

3"

SET POST 2'-0"
DEEP & TAMP.

809

PROTECTIVE FENCE—This one gives you protection with a colorful design. It will keep children in the yard and keep frolicsome dogs out. The gate is sturdy and made in a contemporary design. The center reinforced plastic panel can be a colorful plaque for your home numbers.

Sketches courtesy of Monsanto Chemical Co.

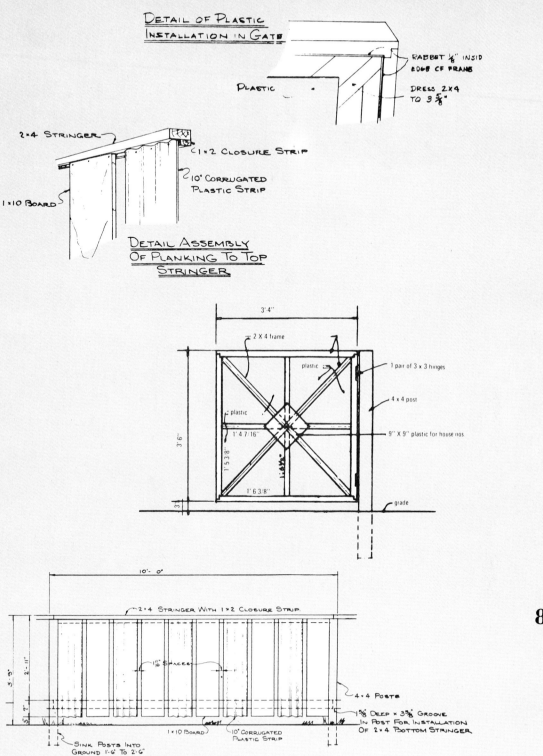

DETAIL OF PLASTIC
INSTALLATION IN GATE

RABBET ⅛" INSID
EDGE OF FRAME

PLASTIC

DRESS 2×4
TO 3⅝"

2×4 STRINGER

1×2 CLOSURE STRIP

10" CORRUGATED
PLASTIC STRIP

1×10 BOARD

DETAIL ASSEMBLY
OF PLANKING TO TOP
STRINGER

3'·4"

2 X 4 frame

plastic

1 pair of 3 x 3 hinges

4 x 4 post

plastic

3'·6"

9" X 9" plastic for house nos

1' 4 7/16"

1' 5 3/8"

1' 6 3/8"

3"

grade

10'- 0"

2×4 STRINGER WITH 1×2 CLOSURE STRIP.

3'·9"

2'-11"

1¹¹⁄₁₆" SPACES

4×4 POSTS

7"

1⅝" DEEP × 3⅜" GROOVE
IN POST FOR INSTALLATION
OF 2×4 BOTTOM STRINGER

1×10 BOARD

10" CORRUGATED
PLASTIC STRIP

SINK POSTS INTO
GROUND 1'-6" TO 2'-6"

811

DECORATIVE FENCE—This fence outlines your property and accents the landscaping in your yard. It's low enough not to cut off the view, but high enough to invite trespassers to walk around.

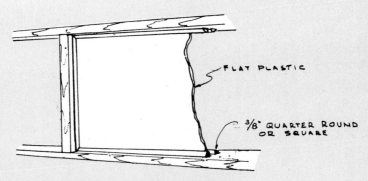

FLAT PLASTIC

3/8" QUARTER ROUND OR SQUARE

DETAIL ASSEMBLY SHOWING INSTALLATION OF PLASTIC

812

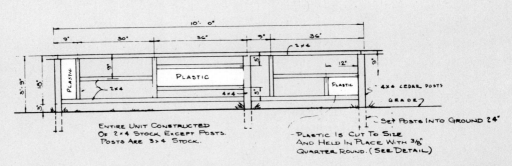

ENTIRE UNIT CONSTRUCTED OF 2×4 STOCK EXCEPT POSTS. POSTS ARE 3×4 STOCK.

PLASTIC IS CUT TO SIZE AND HELD IN PLACE WITH 3/8" QUARTER ROUND. (SEE DETAIL)

Sketches courtesy of Monsanto Chemical Co.

Plywood Fences

On the following pages are detailed step-by-step plans for making a variety of fences out of exterior-grade plywood. There is one to meet your needs and the building style of your home.

Among the plans included are those for a:

1. Saw-tooth or Staggered Wall Fence, particularly useful as a privacy wall or sun shield.

2. Woven Fence made by interlacing 24″ wide strips of plywood.

3. Closed Louver Fence which affords complete privacy and yet because of the louver setting of the panels gives the fence a lighter look.

4. Vertical Venetian Blind Fence for areas where you sometimes want the sun and at other times wish to shut it out.

5. Panel Fence for Carports which can be used to add a decorative finish to your carport and hide the car from view from your outdoor living area.

6. Framed Square Fence where construction is speeded by the use of large sheets of plywood, but the big areas are broken up by adding vertical and horizontal frames.

Finishing Details

After your fence has been completed, you should apply some finish to protect it from the elements.

The best paint for any wood to be exposed to the weather has proved best for exterior plywood as well. High grade exterior house paints of either titanium-lead-zinc or white lead and oil give excellent service on exterior plywood. Avoid paints which set to a hard, brittle film.

1. The initial or prime coat is the most important. This should be brushed on thoroughly as soon as possible after the fence is erected. Use a high grade exterior primer thinned with at least one pint pure raw linseed oil per gallon, or use a high grade aluminum primer.

2. Over the primer coat, following as closely as conditions permit, apply second and third coats according to paint manufacturer's directions, either brushed or sprayed on.

3. Paint both sides of the fence with equal coverage.

Saw-Tooth Fence

1. Indicated on Figure A is a method you can adopt for locating the fence. The plan shows a 4′x8′ offset "step," but you can make this any length you wish by trimming the exterior plywood panels to the desired offset. Make a template out of the batten stock, as shown in figure A for locating the post holes. Posts should be redwood or cedar, although other materials may be used if treated

---

MATERIALS

Exterior-type Douglas Fir plywood—4′ x 8′ x ⅜″ thick
Posts—4″x4″x10′
Intermediate rails—2″x3″x8′
Stops—⅜″x1 1/16″
Battens—1 1/16″x2″x8′
Galvanized nails
    4d for battens
    8d for nailing rails to posts
    16d for nailing top tail to posts
Paint

TOOLS

Hammer
Carpenter's square
Saw
Spirit level or plumb bob
Shovel or post-hole digger
Chalk line
Brush
Six-foot rule or steel tape

813

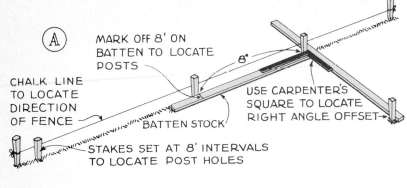

Ⓐ

MARK OFF 8' ON BATTEN TO LOCATE POSTS

CHALK LINE TO LOCATE DIRECTION OF FENCE

8'

USE CARPENTER'S SQUARE TO LOCATE RIGHT ANGLE OFFSET

BATTEN STOCK

STAKES SET AT 8' INTERVALS TO LOCATE POST HOLES

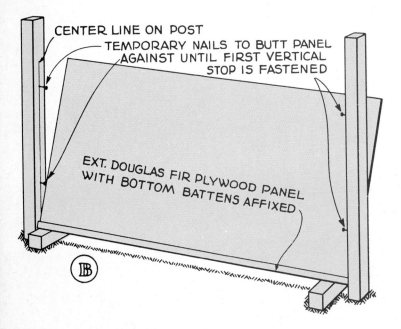

CENTER LINE ON POST

TEMPORARY NAILS TO BUTT PANEL AGAINST UNTIL FIRST VERTICAL STOP IS FASTENED

EXT. DOUGLAS FIR PLYWOOD PANEL WITH BOTTOM BATTENS AFFIXED

Ⓑ

MITRE JOINT

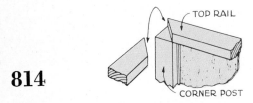

TOP RAIL

CORNER POST

FIG. C

814

or impregnated with wood preservative to assure long life while set in earth. Position each post, using spirit level or plumb bob to set to true vertical. Tamp dirt to pack tightly.

2. Edge-seal the exterior plywood panels with a thick lead and oil paint or other suitable compound. With 4d nails, nail the $1\frac{1}{16}''x2''$ battens horizontally on each side of the bottom of the panel, slightly recessing the panel as shown on Plan 3. Then cut four side stops to fit between batten and the top of the panel.

3. Mark a center line on the inside of each post to locate plywood panel in vertical position. Set the exterior plywood panel on blocks which raise it about 4″ from the ground, positioning it between the posts. Hold panel in place vertically by setting temporary nails in the posts on one side of the panel. (Figure B.) Then nail one stop to each post as shown on Plan 5. Fasten panel to the stops. Remove temporary nails from other side of panel and fasten stops on that side.

4. Cut 2″x3″x8′ intermediate rail. Cut two stops to fit this rail. With 8d nails, toe-nail rail to posts, flush with the top of the panel. Then nail the two stops in place as indicated on Plan 2.

5. Measure 12″ above the 2″x3″ rail and mark each post with a square. Trim posts to this height. Plan shows a 12″ open space. It can be more, or less, if you wish.

Cut and nail the top rail to the posts, with 16d nails. This rail should be centered on intermediate posts. For joining rail at corner posts, miter as shown on Figure C.

6. Nail $1\frac{1}{16}''x2''$ battens vertically in the center on both faces of the panel. Cut a spacer from the 2″x3″ stock to fit between the cap and intermediate rails, then nail in place so it is lined up vertically with battens.

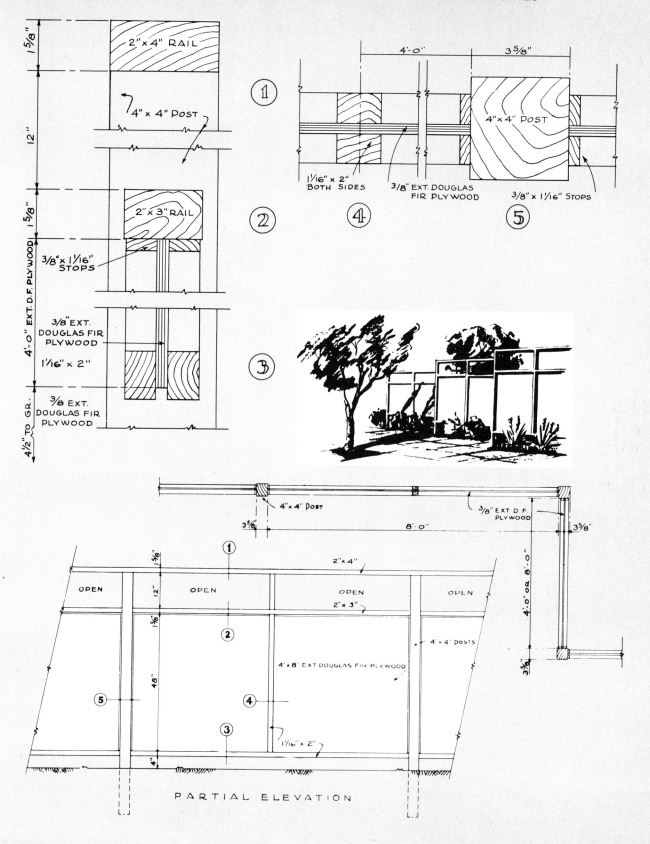

2" x 4" RAIL

4" x 4" POST

2" x 3" RAIL

3/8" x 1 1/16" STOPS

3/8" EXT. DOUGLAS FIR PLYWOOD

1 1/16" x 2"

3/8" EXT. DOUGLAS FIR PLYWOOD

1 5/8"

12"

1 5/8"

4'-0" EXT. D.F. PLYWOOD

4 1/2" TO GR.

① ② ③

4'-0"

3 5/8"

4" x 4" POST

1 1/16" x 2" BOTH SIDES

3/8" EXT. DOUGLAS FIR PLYWOOD

3/8" x 1 1/16" STOPS

④ ⑤

4" x 4" POST

3/8" EXT D.F. PLYWOOD

3 5/8"

8'-0"

3 5/8"

4'-0" OR 8'-0"

3 5/8"

OPEN   OPEN   OPEN   OPEN

2" x 4"

2" x 3"

4" x 4" POSTS

4' x 8' EXT DOUGLAS FIR PLYWOOD

1 1/16" x 2"

1 5/8"

12"

1 5/8"

48"

4"

① ② ③ ④ ⑤

PARTIAL ELEVATION

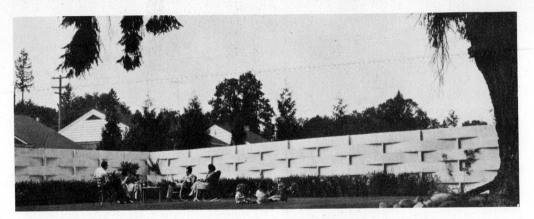

Woven Plywood Fence

1. Locate fence position by stretching chalk line between stakes. Dig the first hole (all holes should be at least 2' deep) and position the first post, using a spirit level or plumb bob to set it to true vertical. Tamp dirt around it to pack tightly.

All posts should be cedar or redwood, although other material may be used if treated or impregnated with wood preservative to assure long life while set in earth.

2. The first and last two posts in

MATERIALS
Exterior-type Douglas fir plywood (Fence is constructed of ¼″ panels 2′ x 8′, cut from standard plywood sheets.)
Posts—4″x4″x10′
Divider posts—2″x4″x6′
6d galvanized casing nails
Paint
TOOLS
Hammer
Saw
Spirit level
Shovel or post-hole digger
Chalk line
Brush

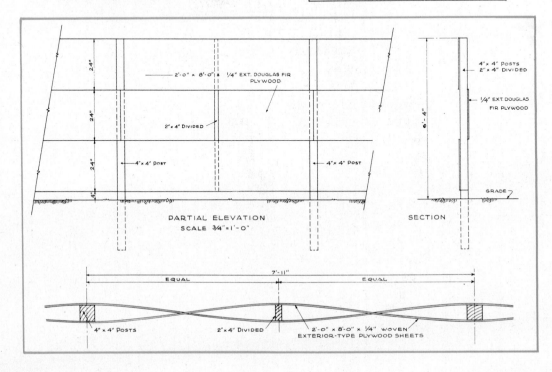

PARTIAL ELEVATION
SCALE ¾″=1′-0″

SECTION

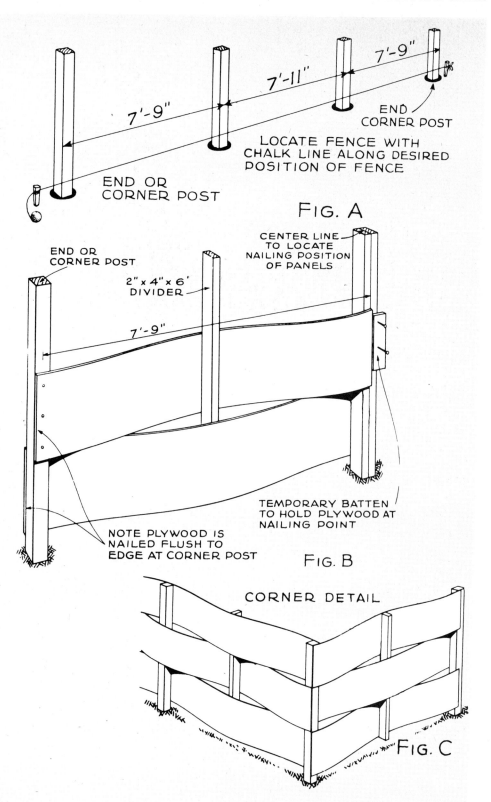

7'-9"

7'-11"

7'-9"

END
CORNER POST

END OR CORNER POST

LOCATE FENCE WITH
CHALK LINE ALONG DESIRED
POSITION OF FENCE

FIG. A

END OR
CORNER POST

CENTER LINE
TO LOCATE
NAILING POSITION
OF PANELS

2" x 4" x 6'
DIVIDER

7'-9"

TEMPORARY BATTEN
TO HOLD PLYWOOD AT
NAILING POINT

NOTE PLYWOOD IS
NAILED FLUSH TO
EDGE AT CORNER POST

FIG. B

CORNER DETAIL

FIG. C

817

any direction are set on 7'9" centers so exterior plywood panels will line up flush with the outside edge of the first and last posts. Remaining posts are set on 7'11" centers. (Figure A.) Mark off and position as many posts as you will need, using a spirit level to set them to true vertical.

3. Mark a center line on the front

and back faces of all the posts except the first or corner post. Nail small temporary battens to these lines. Edge-seal the plywood panels with a thick lead and oil paint or other suitable compound. Nail one panel flush with the edge of the first post, about 4" above the ground. Bend the panel so as to butt against the batten on the corresponding face of the second post, then nail it. (Figure B.)

4. Nail the second plywood panel flush with the edge of the first post, but on the opposite side from the panel just applied. The bottom of this panel rests on top of the first panel. Bend this panel in reverse direction to the first panel, so it butts against the batten on the second post, then nail.

5. Take the 6' divider post and nail vertically between the two panels at their centers as shown on the plans.

6. Position the top panel in the same manner as the bottom panel and nail to the divider post to complete the section, using temporary battens or stops to hold panel in desired nailing position. (Battens are re-used and thrown away when fence is completed; they may be any scrap lumber.) Trim posts flush with the top plywood panel.

Repeat procedure on all remaining fence sections. Figure C shows typical corner detail.

NOTE: An attractive alternate design can be created by using ¼" exterior plywood panels cut to 16" widths. Four to six such widths could be woven into the posts, depending upon height desired. Post and divider lengths would naturally have to be altered to fit planned height.

Closed Louver Fence

MATERIALS
Exterior-type Douglas fir plywood—2'x6'x⅜"
Posts—2"x6"x10'
Intermediate posts—1"x6"x6'
Side rails for base—1"x6", random lengths
Base cap, and cap rail—1"x8"x14'
Quarter round—¾"
Galvanized nails—4d and 8d
Paint
TOOLS
Hammer
Saw
Bevel gauge
Spirit level
Shovel or post-hole digger
Square
Chalk line
Brush

---

1. See Figure A. First, lay out and cut one section of 1"x8" base cap to use as a template to space the posts in the ground, as well as to set them at the proper angle. On this piece actually lay out in pencil, one length of a complete panel assembly consisting of posts, intermediate posts, and three exterior-type plywood panels, as indicated on the plans. Cut this piece of stock on the angles at the inner edge of each 2" guide for setting the posts accurately. As shown on Figure B, marking a center line will be helpful in lining up the template and posts.

2. Locate the fence by stretching a chalk line between two stakes. This line will act as a guide for the back or front of the fence, whichever you

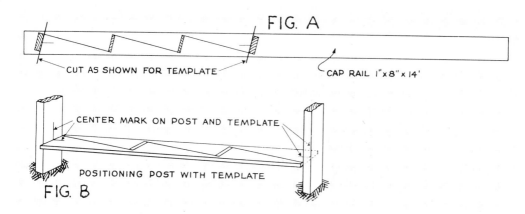

FIG. A

CUT AS SHOWN FOR TEMPLATE   CAP RAIL 1"x8"x14'

CENTER MARK ON POST AND TEMPLATE

POSITIONING POST WITH TEMPLATE

FIG. B

819

Rustic picket fence remains a do-it-your-self favorite. Fence of vertical redwood slats provides a charming backdrop for this lovely backyard garden.

820

prefer. Dig the first hole. All post holes should be at least 2′ deep.

Posts should be cedar or redwood, although other material may be used if treated or impregnated with a wood preservative to assure long life while set in earth.

Take your template and line it up lengthwise with the chalk line, allowing one end of the template to extend a little beyond the inside edge of the post hole. Butt the post to the angle end of the template. Tamp the dirt, holding the post in position. Use a spirit level to set the post vertically.

3. Replace your template again with one end butted to your first positioned post. Dig the next hole at the end of the template for the second

post. Center your second post at the angle of the template; fill in the dirt and tamp. Again, use the spirit level to set the post vertically.

4. Now that you have set the first two posts, proceed with the rest of them, using the template for spacing and setting the posts at the correct angle. If you need a corner, cut the 1″x8″ base as shown in Figure C and use it to position the first post in the other direction. Then position and set the remaining posts with the first template.

5. Apply the rails to the base of the fence. Rails are 1″x6″ stock, random lengths, with scab joints as indicated on Figure D. Nail the rails temporarily, with one nail in each post, so you can do some adjusting later if necessary. Nail the first rail to the front posts about 4″ above the ground. Because the posts are set at an angle, the rails will touch on the corner of each post. Nail another rail to the back of the posts in the same manner, making sure it is at the same level as the first rail. Now, take your template and cut as many pieces of 1″x8″ as are needed to fit between posts to complete the base assembly. Nail each piece to the top of the two side rails between the posts.

6. Trim the posts to the correct height—6″ above the base. Set one of the plywood panels upright on the base and mark the post at the top of the panel. Cut accurately. Figure E is suggested means for supporting the post while you trim it.

7. Next, apply the cap rail to the frame. This is 1″x8″ stock 14′ in length. It will cover two sections of fence. Set the rail in place. Nail it temporarily to the first post, allowing the end of the cap rail to

extend a little beyond the first post. Place your template under the cap rail between the first and second posts to adjust the correct distance at the top. Temporarily nail the cap to the second post. Again, place the template under the cap rail to measure the distance between the second and third rail. Then trim the cap rail on angle at center of third post and temporarily fasten in place.

8. Trim the 1"x6" intermediate posts to the same height as the plywood panels. Edge-seal the plywood with a thick lead and oil paint or suitable compound. Nail the panels to the intermediate posts as indicated on the plans. This unit consists of three plywood panels and two intermediate posts. Position this unit between the base and cap rail. Nail the first plywood panel to the center of the first post; then nail the third plywood panel to the center of the second post. You now have a section in place, and the remaining sections are handled in the same manner.

9. Now that the units fit snugly between the posts, nail quarter-round molding to the cap rail and also the base, flush with the face of the plywood panels. This holds the panels at top and bottom so you can toe-nail them to the cap rail; toe-nail them to the base. Now, permanently nail all frame parts and proceed to the next section.

Alternate Panel Arrangements

If you wish your fence 8' high, simply cut each 4'x8' panel of plywood into two 2'x8' pieces and provide 12' posts for the necessary height. Figure F shows an alternate treatment for a 6' fence, using an

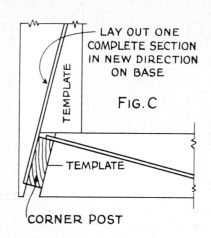

FIG. C

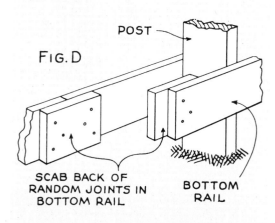

FIG. D

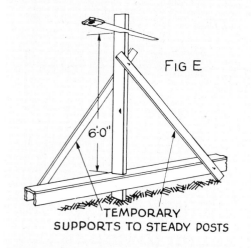

FIG E

821

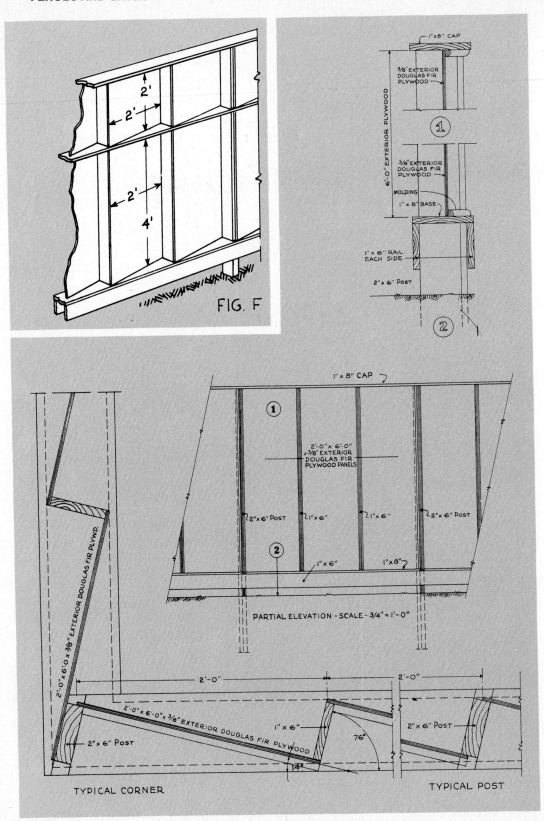

FIG. F

1"x8" CAP

3/8" EXTERIOR
DOUGLAS FIR
PLYWOOD

6'-0" EXTERIOR PLYWOOD

3/8" EXTERIOR
DOUGLAS FIR
PLYWOOD

MOLDING

1" x 8" BASE

1" x 6" RAIL
EACH SIDE

2" x 6" POST

1"x 8" CAP

2'-0"x 6'-0"
x3/8" EXTERIOR
DOUGLAS FIR
PLYWOOD PANELS

2"x6" POST   1"x 6"   1"x 6"   2" x 6" POST

1"x 6"   1"x 8"

PARTIAL ELEVATION - SCALE - 3/4" = 1'-0"

822

2'-0"x 6'-0 x 3/8" EXTERIOR DOUGLAS FIR PLYW'D.

2'-0"

2'-0"

2'-0"x 6'-0"x 3/8" EXTERIOR DOUGLAS FIR PLYWOOD

1" x 6"

76°

2" x 6" POST

2" x 6" POST

14°

TYPICAL CORNER

TYPICAL POST

intermediate rail and 4'x8' plywood panels. Here, cut the 4'x8' panels into 2'x8' pieces for the bottom and 2'x2' for the top portion of each fence section.

Vertical Venetian Blind Fence

1. First you will have to figure the opening you wish to fill with the movable screen sections. Then divide the total space to determine how many sections will be needed, remembering that the total width of any one section will be a maximum of 4'2", the total height a maximum of 8'4¼".

2. After dividing the opening to determine the total number of sections needed, construct the framework for the sections. Framing is 2"x3", rabbeted to accommodate the plywood panel (⅜" wide and ⅝" deep) as shown on Figure A. Size of the opening will naturally determine the size of each section.

3. Miter frame corners as shown in Figure B. Glue and nail the corner joint. Fit panel into the rabbeted frame and toe-nail with 6d galvanized nails. Seal edges of the plywood panels with a thick lead and oil paint or other suitable compound. Set the bottom panel—frame joint in mastic to prevent water from entering joint and injuring paint finish.

4. Mark off center of each door frame, top and bottom, for pivots upon which door will swing. Figure shows a simple pivot you can construct with ½" threaded pipe. It is suggested that a foot-type door stop be used for holding each door at any desired position.

```
MATERIALS
    Exterior-type Douglas fir Ply-
        wood—4'x8'x⅜" thick
    Framing Material—2"x3"
    Galvanized casing nails
    Hardware as shown
    Waterproof-type glue
    Mastic
    Paint
TOOLS
    Carpenters' square
    Rule
    Brace and bits
    Miter-box
    Saw, hammer
    Sandpaper, brush
```

(cont. p. 824)

823

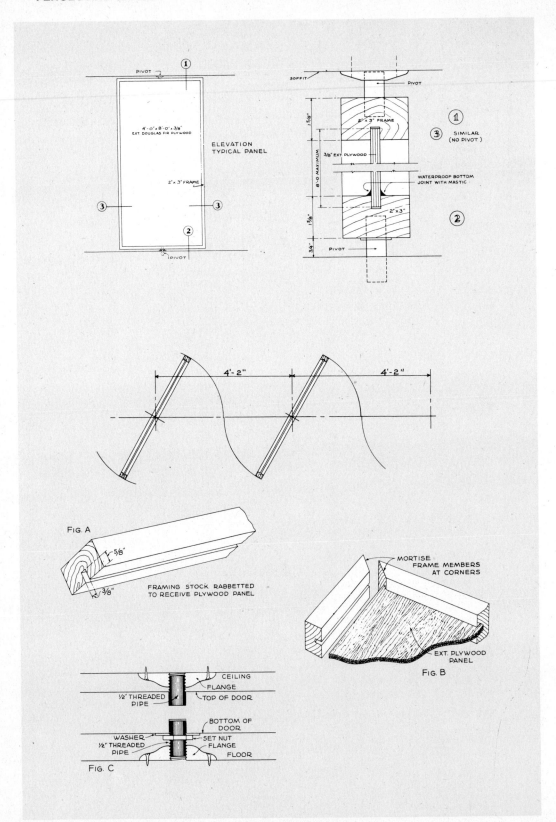

PIVOT

4'-0" x 8'-0" x 3/8"
EXT. DOUGLAS FIR PLYWOOD

ELEVATION
TYPICAL PANEL

2" x 3" FRAME

③   ③

②

PIVOT

SOFFIT

PIVOT

2" x 3" FRAME

①

③ SIMILAR
(NO PIVOT)

3/8" EXT. PLYWOOD

WATERPROOF BOTTOM
JOINT WITH MASTIC

2" x 3"

②

PIVOT

4'-2"   4'-2"

FIG. A

5/8"

3/8"

FRAMING STOCK RABBETTED
TO RECEIVE PLYWOOD PANEL

MORTISE
FRAME MEMBERS
AT CORNERS

EXT. PLYWOOD
PANEL

FIG. B

CEILING
FLANGE
TOP OF DOOR
1/2" THREADED
PIPE

BOTTOM OF
DOOR
WASHER   SET NUT
1/2" THREADED   FLANGE
PIPE   FLOOR

FIG. C

824

Carport Fence

1. If your carport is already supported by posts you can of course apply the exterior-type plywood panels horizontally to these posts, cap the top and place the rail at the bottom as shown above. If your port is a wide soffit or overhang, or has supports only at the extreme corners,

you will need to place posts properly on 4′ center as outlined in step 2.

```
MATERIALS
    Exterior-type Douglas fir ply-
      wood panels—4′x8′x⅜″
    Posts—4″x4″
    Horizontal rail strips—1″x2″
    6d Galvanized nails
    Steel tape or rule
    Paint
```

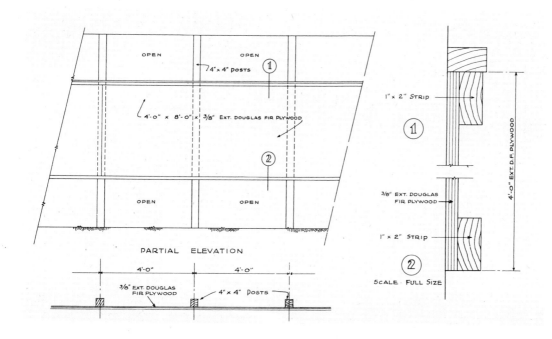

PARTIAL ELEVATION

825

2. Intermediate posts to support the plywood panels are best set on concrete blocks, shimmed to proper height so post can be nailed to framing member on underside of the carport roof. Set posts on 4′ centers.

3. Seal edges of the plywood panels with a thick lead and oil paste or other suitable compound. Place the standard 4′x8′ panels on the posts, midway between the ground and the underside of the carport roof-line. Panels are nailed to posts with 6d galvanized nails.

4. When panels are in place, nail a 1″x3″ batten flush with the top of the panel as shown on Drawing 1 of the plans. Do the same with the bottom of the panel, as shown on Drawing 2.

5. Across the top of the panel and the top batten just applied, nail another 1″x2″ batten, allowing it to extend beyond the first batten. (See Drawing 1.) This carries out a horizontal effect and gives a finished appearance to the job.

ALTERNATE DESIGN ARRANGEMENTS

You can vary the basic suggested design in many ways to create individual, distinctive effects. Here in sketch form are five additional ideas for panel arrangement and decorative treatment.

826

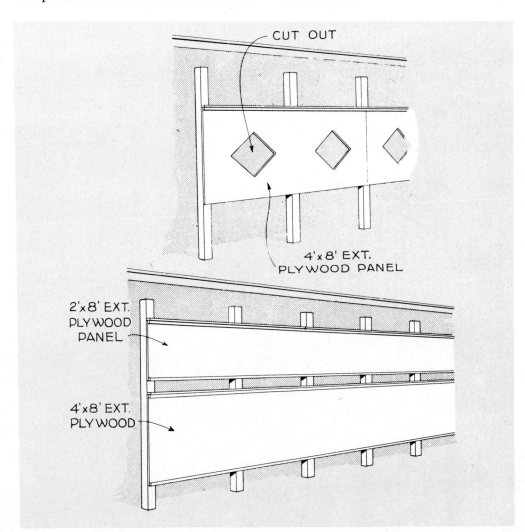

CUT OUT

4′ x 8′ EXT. PLYWOOD PANEL

2′x8′ EXT. PLYWOOD PANEL

4′x8′ EXT. PLYWOOD

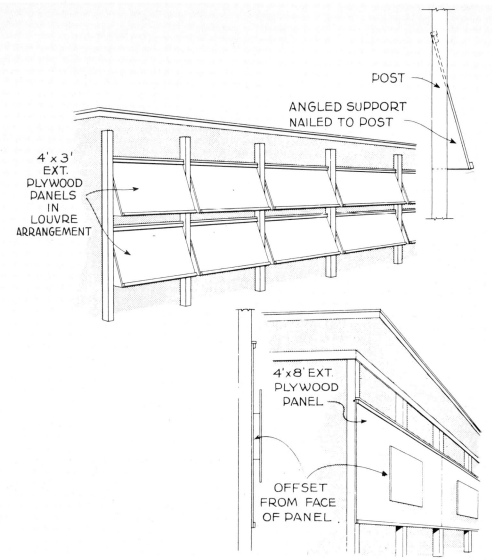

POST

ANGLED SUPPORT
NAILED TO POST

4' x 3'
EXT.
PLYWOOD
PANELS
IN
LOUVRE
ARRANGEMENT

4' x 8' EXT.
PLYWOOD
PANEL

OFFSET
FROM FACE
OF PANEL.

827

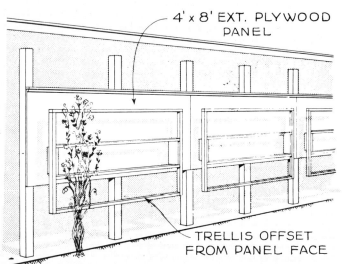

4' x 8' EXT. PLYWOOD
PANEL

TRELLIS OFFSET
FROM PANEL FACE

Framed Squares

1. Locate fence by stretching a chalk line between two stakes, then dig your post holes at least 2' deep, spaced 4' apart. Posts should be cedar or redwood, although other material may be used if treated or impregnated with wood preservative to insure long life while set in earth.

2. As indicated on plan, 2"x4" intermediate posts will have a 2"x4" scab nailed on them, from ground line down. Seal between post and scab with thick lead and oil paint, aluminum paint, or high-grade exterior house primer. This gives added protection against deterioration. Cut a 2"x4" four feet long to use as a spacer to position each post. Tamp the dirt tightly around the post. Use a spirit level or plumb bob to set post on true vertical. (Figure A.)

3. Edge-seal the plywood panels with a thick lead and oil paint or other suitable compound. Nail 1"x2" batten horizontally on both sides of the panel at the bottom, slightly recessing the panel as shown in Figure B. Cut four 1"x1" stops to fit between this batten and the top of the panel.

4. Find center of each post and

828

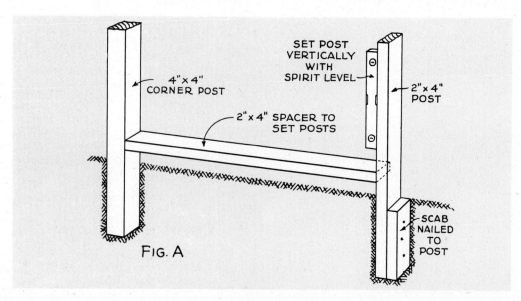

FIG. A

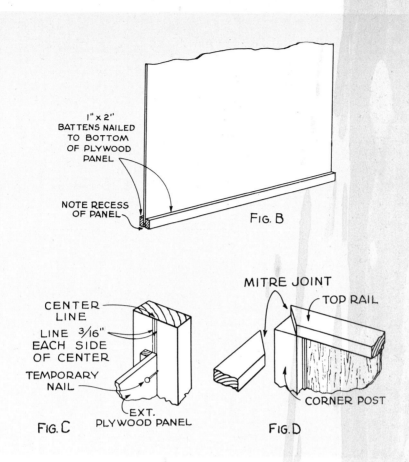

1"x2" BATTENS NAILED TO BOTTOM OF PLYWOOD PANEL

NOTE RECESS OF PANEL

FIG. B

CENTER LINE

LINE 3/16" EACH SIDE OF CENTER

TEMPORARY NAIL

FIG. C

EXT. PLYWOOD PANEL

MITRE JOINT

TOP RAIL

CORNER POST

FIG. D

draw two lines, each ³⁄₁₆″ from this center line, which will show nailing position of panel on post. Position the panel between posts by setting it on blocks which will hold it about 4″ above ground line. Set the panel in place, using temporary nails as stops on one side until the vertical 1″x1″ stop is in place on opposite side. (See Figure C.) Remove temporary nails and nail opposite stop to post, then to panel.

5. Trim posts flush with top of the panel. Cut and nail the top rail to the posts. Top rail should be flush with the outside of the first and last post. Joints in top rail should be planned to come on center of any intermediate post, depending on length of top rails used. For joining rail to 4″x4″ corner post, miter as shown in Figure D.

6. Cut two more 1″x1″ stops. Position them to hold the plywood panel in place under top rail. (See Plan 1.) Nail 1″x2″ battens to quarter the panel faces on both sides. (See Plan 2.)

NOTE: If one section of fence is to be used for shelves, as suggested, these shelves can be made from ¾″ exterior-type plywood. Decorative shapes can easily be cut with a jigsaw, if desired. If valances are wanted (as shown in Figure E), these may be cut from ⅜″ exterior plywood.

(Cont. p. 830)

829

MATERIALS

Exterior-type Douglas fir plywood. Fence is constructed of ⅜" thick panels 4'x6', which should be cut from standard plywood sheets.

Corner posts—4"x4"x10'

Extra 2"x4" for below ground scabs on posts

Intermediate posts—2"x4"x 10'

Stops—1"x1"

Battens—1"x2"

Galvanized nails—
  16d for top rail
  8d for bottom rail
  4d for battens and stops

Paint

TOOLS

Saw

Shovel or post-hole digger

Chalk line

Plumb bob or level

Brush

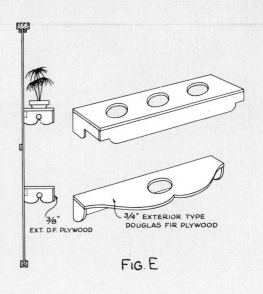

FIG. E

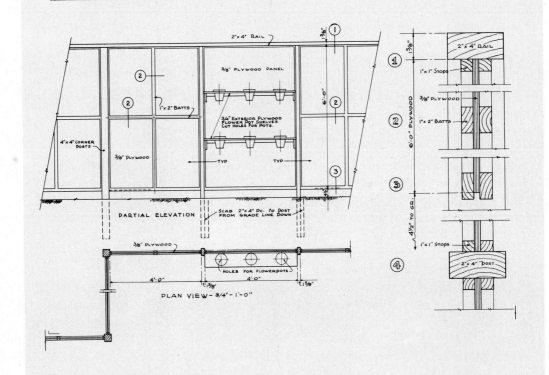

Fertilizers

Materials

For convenience and adequate turf nutrition, use a complete fertilizer; that is, a fertilizer containing all three of the major fertilizer materials. The law requires that every package of fertilizer be labelled to show the guaranteed minimum percentages (or grade) of the three important fertilizer nutrients. For example, a 10-6-4 fertilizer contains at least 10% nitrogen, 6% phosphoric acid, and 4% potash. Many grades of complete fertilizer are available.

Most complete fertilizers are composed of simple chemicals quickly absorbed by plants. These inorganic fertilizers are the least expensive, but they require some care for safe application during the growing season. Natural organic fertilizer (such as activated sludge, processed tankage, and vegetable meals) release their nutrients somewhat more slowly. They are more expensive but they will not burn growing grass even if they are applied carelessly. Otherwise, the effect of the two types of fertilizer is similar, especially where clippings are left on the lawn.

Barnyard manure is not a good lawn fertilizer, for it is relatively low in nutrients and usually contains large numbers of weed seeds. Weed-free fertilizers are to be preferred, even when manure can be had without cost. Commercially dried manures are relatively expensive for the benefits received.

Liquid fertilizers may be more convenient to apply than dry fertilizers under certain circumstances. This is their only advantage over

Photograph courtesy of O M Scott & Sons
Dry fertilizers, which can be applied by hand, are best applied with a spreader.

equivalent amounts of the more economical dry fertilizers.

Fertilizing Established Turf

If yours is an average lawn in good condition, fertilize it in early fall. If your soil is poor, repeat the application in early spring. Even on good soils this second application will do no harm.

Rates to Use

The fertilizer recommendations given here are in terms of pounds of 5-10-5 or its equivalent, only because 5-10-5 is widely available at competitive prices and often is at hand for other purposes. Some other complete fertilizer may be more economical for you, depending upon your local market conditions; or perhaps you will choose a natural organic fertilizer or a combination organic-inorganic fertilizer because it is safer to apply to growing grass and stimulates the grass somewhat more gradually. So far as the benefit to the grass is concerned, any of the many common grades of complete fertilizer will be satisfactory so long as you use it at the proper rate.

To determine the proper rate for a single application of any fertilizer, consider only the first figure (nitrogen) of the grade you have chosen. Then find the rate for 1,000 square feet as listed in the table.

How to Apply

Apply fertilizers evenly, or your lawn will have dark and light streaks. A mechanical spreader is best for this work. You may apply a natural organic fertilizer at any season without danger of burning your grass. Inorganic fertilizers will not burn if you spread them in early spring before growth starts. Inorganic fertilizers are entirely practical during the growing season, also, but take these precautions against burning: be especially careful about even distribution;

Amount of Fertilizer To Use		
	For 1,000 square feet of area	
If the first figure of the grade is	of established lawn	of new seed-bed or lawn to be renovated
	Pounds	Pounds
4	25	50
5	20	40
6	17	33
7	14	28
8	12½	25
9	11	22
10	10	20

spread fertilizer only when the grass is completely dry; and sprinkle the lawn thoroughly to wash the fertilizer from the grass blades to the ground.

How to Use Liquid Fertilizers

If you want to grow big plants fast, you can't beat the new soluble fertilizers. Because they are liquid, they get to the plant in less time and produce results more quickly. You can sprinkle them right onto the leaves—dry fertilizer would "burn" if applied that way—for fastest action, or you can pour them on the ground around the plant. They work fine on everything from African violet house plants to lawns and shade trees.

Besides making your garden grow faster, liquid fertilizers are a lot more convenient to use. You can save work by combining fertilizing with other spraying or sprinkling chores. Lawns and many flowers can get their feedings as part of a regular watering.

If you spray fruit trees with DDT, you can mix fertilizer into the insecticide solution and feed the tree while you kill the bugs.

832

Several brands of ready-to-dissolve fertilizers are on the market, but you can reduce the cost by mixing your own. You need three chemicals: potassium nitrate (saltpeter), monoammonium phosphate and urea. All three of these chemicals supply nitrogen, while the ammonium phosphate also supplies phosphorus and the potassium nitrate gives potassium.

You can buy these chemicals from laboratory- or chemical-supply houses in most cities. Ask for "technical" or "fertilizer" grades which are cheaper.

How to Mix

Different plants require different proportions of the three plant-food elements—leafy plants need lots of nitrogen, root crops don't. Formulas for three common mixtures are given in an accompanying table (the numbers indicate the percentages of nitrogen, phosphoric oxide and potassium oxide, respectively). Other ratios are easily obtained. Equal volumes will give a 21-21-18 fertilizer, while equal weights make a 23-20-15 fertilizer. If you have no scale for weights, measure by volume (see table).

The actual mixing is best done by dumping the dry chemicals onto newspaper and turning the stuff over and over with your hands. It must be completely and evenly mixed because you will later want to scoop out a spoonful or cupful of properly proportioned fertilizer. Another way is to dissolve the dry chemicals—unmixed—into a concentrated solution.

Three Formulas for Mixing Soluble Plant Foods

Balanced fertilizer

(Approx. analysis, 20-20-20)	1-lb. batch	10-lb. batch
Potassium nitrate	7 oz. (¾ cup)	4¼ lb. (7½ cups)
Urea	4 oz. (⅔ cup)	2½ lb. (7 cups)
Monoammonium phosphate	5 oz. (⅔ cup)	3¼ lb. (6½ cups)

High-nitrogen fertilizer

(Approx. analysis, 24-17-16)		
Potassium nitrate	5½ oz. (⅝ cup)	3½ lb. (6⅛ cups)
Urea	6 oz. (1 cup)	3¾ lb. (10¼ cups)
Monoammonium phosphate	4½ oz. (⅝ cup)	2¾ lb. (5½ cups)

High-phosphorus fertilizer

(Approx. analysis, 19-23-17)		
Potassium nitrate	6 oz. (⅔ cup)	3¾ lb. (6½ cups)
Urea	4 oz. (⅔ cup)	2½ lb. (7 cups)
Monoammonium phosphate	6 oz. (¾ cup)	3¾ lb. (7½ cups)

Note: The analysis figures indicate approximate percentages of nitrogen, phosphorus and potassium, respectively, in the fertilizer mix. To mix, use the equivalent volume of each ingredient if you don't have a scale.

Sprinkle, pour or spray it—you can choose among three ways of applying liquid fertilizer. When it is sprinkled, leaves absorb some. Pour solution (center) into the ground when transplanting. The hose attachment (right) feeds a lawn while it is being watered.

Healthy lawns don't just happen—feeding with fertilizer is just as important as part of the regular lawn care program as are watering and mowing. The house is the birthplace of Luther Burbank, America's most noted horticulturist.

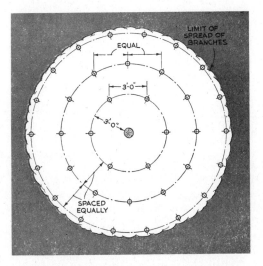

To feed a tree, punch holes in the ground in the pattern shown, pour in liquid fertilizer and then fill the holes with soil.

How to Apply

You have to dissolve the dry mix in water before using. It is concentrated and will burn your plants if applied dry.

The standard-strength solution takes ⅛ pound (¼ cup) of mixed fertilizer to a 12-quart pail of water. For larger or smaller amounts of the standard-strength solution, use these proportions: one teaspoon to one quart of water; one heaping tablespoon to a gallon; ¼ pound (½ cup) to six gallons; one pound (two cups) to 25 gallons.

For garden plants—flowers, vegetables and shrubs — sprinkle the standard-strength solution directly onto the leaves from a watering can, applying it about every two weeks. Large garden areas can be treated with one pound of the fertilizer (25 gallons of solution) per 1,000 square feet. On potted plants and window boxes, substitute the fertilizer solution for the regular watering once every two weeks.

Some house plants, such as African violets and gloxinias, are too delicate for leaf-feeding. Instead, apply a half-strength solution to the soil around the plant every two weeks in place of the regular watering.

For transplanting, use a double-strength solution, but do not apply it directly to the plants. Use it to saturate the soil around the roots. Follow with supplemental leaf-feedings of standard-strength solution every two weeks or so if shrubs look sickly after they have been transplanted.

Trees can be fed with standard-strength solution shortly after they have leafed out. Pour the solution—a gallon or more, depending on the size of the tree—into holes poked in the ground. The holes should be an inch or two in diameter, about 12 inches deep, and spaced two or three feet apart from the trunk to the outermost spread of the branches. After the fertilizer has soaked in, fill the holes back up with earth.

Lawns are almost shamefully easy to feed with liquid fertilizer—attachments for your garden hose let you fertilize and water at the same time. One type of attachment is an "aspirator," a long tube that sucks fertilizer solution from a pail and mixes it with the sprinkling water. Another type works much the same way but takes the fertilizer solution from a small jar connected to a nozzle that you fit to the end of your hose.

Since the fertilizer is greatly diluted when mixed with sprinkling water, you can use an extra-strong solution: one pound of dry mixture to 10 or 12 quarts of water. This is too concentrated to be applied directly to the lawn and should be used only with a hose attachment.

Use about one pound of fertilizer for each 2,000 square feet of lawn, applying it every two or three weeks. New lawns will require more feeding—say once a week—to get started. In hot, dry weather fertilize less often.

Files

Files and rasps have three distinguishing features:

(1) Their length, which is always measured exclusive of the tang.

(2) Their kind (or name), which has reference to the shape or style.

(3) Their cut, which has reference to both the character and the relative degrees of coarseness of the teeth.

Length—The length of the file is the distance between its heel (or part of the file where the tang begins) and the point (or end opposite). The tang (or portion of the file prepared for the reception of the handle) is never included in the length. In general, the length of files bears no fixed proportion to either their width or their thickness, even though the files be of the same kind.

Kind—By kind is meant the various shapes or styles of files, as distinguished by such technical names as Flat, Mill, Half Round, etc. These are divided, from the form of their cross-sections, into three general geometrical classes: Quadrangular, Circular and Triangular. From them are derived, further, odd and irregular forms or cross-sections which are classified as Miscellaneous. These sections, in turn, are sub-divided, according to their general contour or outline, into *taper* and *blunt*.

• *Taper* designates a file, the point of which is more or less reduced in size (both width and thickness) by a gradually narrowing section extending from one-half to two-thirds the length of the file, from the point.

• *Blunt* designates a file that preserves its *sectional size throughout,* from point to tang.

Cut—The cut of files is divided, with reference to the character of the teeth, into single, double, rasp and curved; and with reference to the coarseness of the teeth, into coarse bastard, second and smooth cuts.

Single cut files are usually used with a light pressure to produce a smooth surface finish, or a keen edge on a knife, shears, saw-tooth or other cutting implement.

Double cut files are usually used, under heavier pressure, for fast metal removal and where a rougher finish is permissible.

Rasp cut is a series of individual teeth produced by a sharp, narrow, punch-like cutting chisel. It is an extremely rough cut and is used principally on wood, leather, aluminum, lead, and similarly soft substances for fast removal of material.

Photographs courtesy of Nicholson File Co.

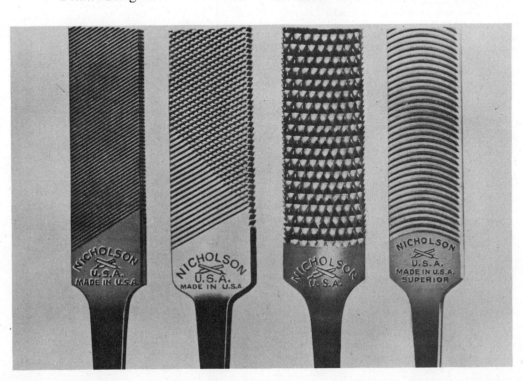

The accompanying illustration shows a typical range of coarseness of tapered and blunt mill files. These also apply approximately to the triangular and other shapes of saw files.

Mill File (Tapered) with square edges. Also made with one or two round edges for filing the gullets between saw teeth.

Mill File (Blunt) or Special Crosscut with square edges.

Triangular Saw Files (Tapered) are made for filing all types of saws with teeth of 60° angle. Various thicknesses; taper, extra slim taper, double extra slim taper.

Triangular Saw Files (Blunt) are frequently preferred by carpenters and other expert filers of 60° hand-saws. Various thicknesses. Cantsaw File is used for sharpening saws with less than 60° angle teeth—for many types of circulars and also for crosscuts with "M" teeth.

Crosscut File is used for sharpening a great variety of crosscut saws. Rounded back is used to deepen gullets of saw teeth; sides for filing teeth themselves.

837

Pruning Saw File is specially designed for use on needle point pruning saws. Single cut on edges and both faces of one side; other side uncut.

Mill Files

Mill files are so named because they are widely used for sharpening mill or circular saws. These files are also useful for sharpening large crosscut saws and mowing-machine knives: for lathe work, drawfiling; for working on compositions of brass and bronze; and for smooth-finish filing in general.

Mill files are single cut and are tapered slightly in width and thickness for about a third of their length. Usually made with two square edges, with cuts thereon as well as on sides. Also made with one and two round edges—to prevent causing sharp corners or edges in the gullets of crosscut saws. The Mill Blunt is likewise used for crosscut saws (and often for bucksaws) as well as for general filing.

Rasp

The rasp cut differs from both the single and double cuts of files in the respect that the teeth are individually formed and disconnected from each other. In the wood rasps the curved side is similar to that of the half round file, but in the cabinet and the patternmakers' rasps, the radius is larger. Rasps are also made in flat and round shapes.

Rasps have long been an important tool of cabinetmakers and handymen working on relatively soft substances requiring the fast removal of material.

Use the Right File

Actually there are thousands of kinds, cuts and sizes of files. That is because there are thousands of different filing jobs, each of which can be done better by using the right file for the job.

Therein lies the first rule on how to get the most out of files. The right file enables the job to be done properly, whereas the wrong one does not —and may, in fact, ruin the work.

The right file saves time, because it performs correctly, and usually faster, on the kind of metal or work for which it is designed.

The right file permits a greater number of efficient filing strokes—

Wood rasps are used by wood workers, wheelwrights and plumbers. Made in flat, half round and round shapes.

Cabinet rasps, used by cabinetmakers and woodworkers, are half round and round, and in same style of cut as wood rasps, but with relatively smaller degrees of coarseness.

Horse rasps come in plain and tanged types and flat section. Plain horse rasps are double ended; all have rasp teeth on one side and file teeth on the other.

838

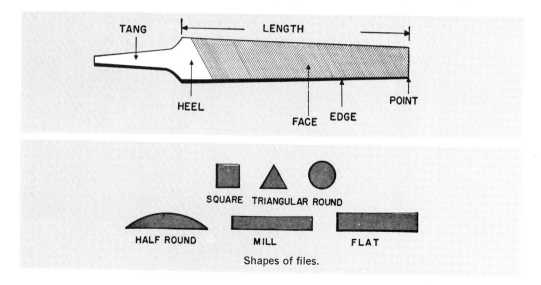

Shapes of files.

per file and per file cost. Sum up all these advantages and they represent a big item of savings.

Many factors enter into the selection of the right file for the job. In general, it may be said that different files are required:

(1) to file a flat or convex surface

(2) to file a curved or concave surface

(3) to file an edge

(4) to file a notch, a slot, or a square or round hole.

But these factors can immediately become complicated by:

(1) the kind of metal or other material to be filed

(2) the kind, shape and hardness of the object or part to be filed

(3) the location, size and character of the surface, edge, notch, slot, or hole to be filed

(4) the amount of metal to be removed—and the practical time permitted for removing it

(5) the degree of smoothness or accuracy required.

All these conditions have a bearing on the kind, size and cut of file which will best attain a particular objective. Calculate the number of possible combinations of such conditions, and selecting exactly the right file for any combination thereof would seem to be a sizable task for any one person.

Experience is a good guide—but a slow teacher. But with proper information, no file user need ever be far off the track to the right file for the job. This, at any rate, is true as to the kind or type of file for the object and metal or other material to be filed. The filer's own survey of the conditions will help further to determine the right size and cut of file.

Use the Right Method

There are three fundamental ways in which a file can be put to work:

1. Straight filing, which consist of pushing the file lengthwise— straight ahead or slightly diagonally —across the work (since all files, with the exception of a few machine operated files, are designed primarily to cut on the forward stroke).

2. Drawfiling, which consists of

839

WRONG

RIGHT

grasping the file at each end and pushing and drawing it across the work.

3. Lathe filing, which consists of stroking the file against work revolved in a lathe.

Place Work at Proper Height

Most work to be filed should be held in a vise. For general filing, the vise should be about elbow height. If a great deal of heavy filing is to be done, it is well to have the work lower. If the work is of a fine or delicate nature, it should be raised near to the eye level.

For work which is apt to become damaged by pressure when held in a vise, it is well to provide a pair of protectors—pieces of zinc, copper, or other fairly soft metal for placing between the jaws and the work to be held. For holding varying sizes of round pieces—such as small rods and pins—a block of hard, close-grained wood with a series of varying-sized grooves is sometimes used where a lot of filing of such pieces is required.

Grasping the File

With files intended for operation with both hands, one of the most generally accepted ways of grasping the handle is to allow its end to fit into and bring up against the fleshy part of the palm below the joint of the little finger—with the thumb lying parallel along the top of the handle and the fingers pointing upward toward the operator's face.

The point of the file is usually grasped by the thumb and the first two fingers of the other hand. The hand may then be held so as to bring the thumb, as its ball presses up on the top of the file, in line with the handle when heavy strokes are required.

When a light stroke is wanted and the pressure demanded be-

840

comes less, the thumb and fingers of the point-holding hand may change their direction until the thumb lies at right angle, or nearly so, with the length of the file—the positions changing more or less as may be needed to increase the downward pressure.

In holding the file with one hand, as in filing pins, dies and edged tools not held in a vise, the forefinger—instead of the thumb—is generally placed on top and as nearly as possible in the direction of its length.

"Carrying" the File

The most natural movement of the hands and arms is to "carry" (stroke) the file across the work in curved lines. This tends toward a rocking motion and, consequently, produces a convex surface where a level surface is desired.

For the usual flat filing, the operator should aim to carry the file forward on an almost straight line—changing its course enough to prevent "grooving."

Keep the File Cutting

One of the quickest ways to ruin a good file is to use too much pressure—or too little—on the forward stroke. Different materials, of course, require different touches; but, in general, just enough pressure should be applied to keep the file cutting at all times. If allowed to slide over the harder metals, the teeth of the file rapidly become dull; and if they are "overloaded" by too much pressure, they are likely to chip or clog.

On the reverse stroke it is best to lift the file clear off the work, ex-

Use protective jaws on vise to protect the work to be filed.

841

cept on very soft metals. Even then the pressure should be very light— never more than the weight of the file itself.

Filing Aluminum

Because aluminum is a soft, ductile and malleable metal, it is difficult to file with ordinary files because the file teeth soon become clogged—even under moderate pressure.

The filing of aluminum can be divided into three general classifications: (1) filing the roughness from aluminum castings; (2) filing sheet and bar aluminum; (3) filing aluminum alloys.

For fast, rough metal removal, a special aluminum rasp is often used. But for cutting aluminum rapidly, yet leaving a good finish, the

Brass is a difficult metal to file and you should use a special file for the job.

Drawfiling consists of grasping the file firmly at both ends and alternately pushing and pulling it sidewise across the work.

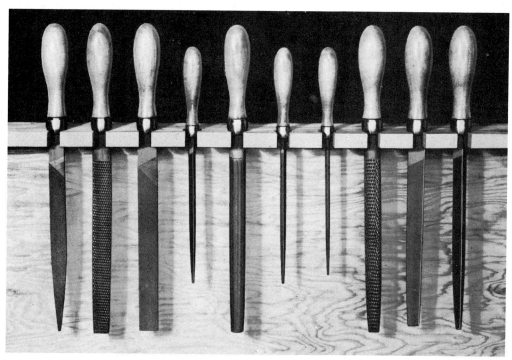

Photograph courtesy of Nicholson File Co.

aluminum "Type A" file is a recent file-manufacturing development. Its special tooth construction is very effective in eliminating clogging. The upcut is deep with an "open-throat"; the overcut fine, producing small scallops on the upcut which break up the filings, allow the file to clear itself, overcome chatter and prevent taking too large a bite.

By using this file with a shearing stroke toward the left, a good finish can easily be obtained.

Files should never be stacked against each other. Keep them separate—standing with their tangs in a row of holes or hung on a rack by their handles as shown.

To set a file in a handle, do not hammer the file! Set end into handle and pound on bench.

Filing Brass

With a structure all its own, brass is a difficult metal to file. While softer than steel, brass is tough and ductile. These characteristics demand file teeth that are sturdy, very sharp, and cut at an angle that prevents "grooving" and running the file off the work. Still more important, the file must not clog.

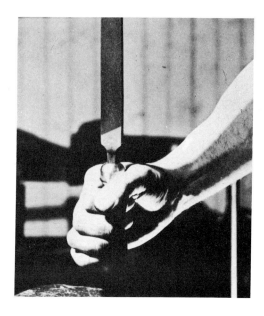

In addition to a short upcut angle, the brass file (like the aluminum "Type A") has a fine, long-angle overcut—producing small scallops which break up the filings and enable the file to clear itself of chips. With a little pressure, the sharp, high-cut teeth bite deep; with less pressure, their short upcut angle produces a smoothing effect.

Filing Lead

Extra-soft metals, such as lead, babbitt and pure copper, present filing conditions distinct from any others herein before described. The

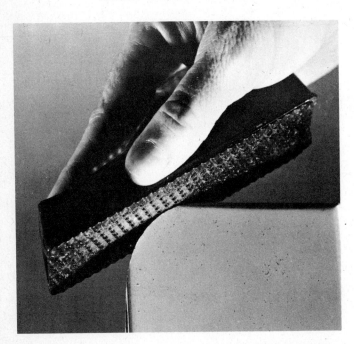

Not a file in the conventional sense, this unusual tool, part of a line called Surform, has teeth resembling a rasp. The teeth are actually deformed openings in sheet steel with extremely sharp, hard cutting edges. Because they are open, they cannot clog, and because they are so tough, they can cut materials such as ceramic tile.

Photos courtesy The Stanley Works

metal removal in normal filing jobs is virtually a "shaving" or "floating" principle, as the design of this lead float file indicates. Its course, short-angle single-cut teeth are virtually a series of stubby blades which shear away the metal rapidly under ordinary pressure. Light pressure produces the smooth effect.

Lead float files are used largely on lead pipe fitting, solder joints and on soft bearings, shims and molded parts.

The Care of Files

File life is greatly shortened by improper care as well as by improper use—and improper selection. Files should never be thrown into a drawer or tool box containing other tools or objects. They should never be laid on top of or stacked

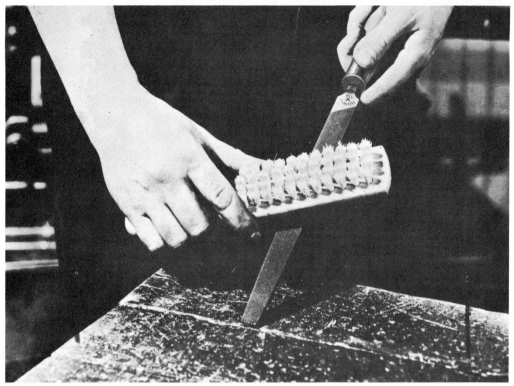

Photograph courtesy of Nicholson File Co.

Clean your files immediately after you've finished working—don't put them away dirty if you expect them to last.

against each other. Such treatment ruins the cutting edges of their teeth. Keep them separate—standing with their tangs in a row of holes or hung on a rack by their handles. Keep them in a dry place so rust will not corrode their teeth.

It is also of great importance to keep files clean of filings or chips, which often collect between the teeth during use. After every few strokes the good mechanic taps the end of the file on the bench to loosen these chips. And he always has on hand a file card or brush. The teeth of the file should be brushed frequently with this type of cleaner, and always before putting the file away. Oil or grease on file should be removed with chalk.

Finger Joint

Technically, a joint with five tongues or fingers on each piece often used on table brackets. The fingers interlock to form the joint.

It is described completely in the section on *DOVETAIL JOINT*.

A modified finger joint—several tongues or fingers are used in place of the normal five.

845

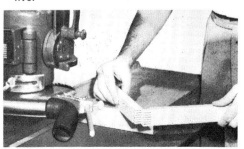

Fire Protection

Any discussion of protection against fire should start with the best way of preventing a fire from getting started. The following suggestions are intended as a general guide for the prevention of fire in the home:

1. Keep matches out of the reach of young children. Teach children the dangers of playing with fire.

2. Do not throw away cigars, cigarettes, and matches without first making sure they are extinguished.

3. Do not allow accumulations of combustible waste materials in or near the house. Without them fires from carelessly discarded materials would be less frequent.

4. Keep chimneys and stovepipes clean with all joints and connections tight. Provide separate metal cans for ashes and rubbish. Never mix the two.

5. Place substantial fire-resistant guards in front of all woodwork close to sources of heat.

6. Keep greasy and oily rags in tightly closed, preferably metal, containers provided for the purpose.

7. Avoid the filling of lighted kerosene and gasoline lamps. Avoid the use of kerosene to start fires in stoves, etc.

8. Do not use gasoline, naptha, or benzine for cleaning. Choose some of the safer solutions now obtainable, and use these, in any considerable quantity, only out-of-doors and during the day.

9. Keep all open flames away from gas leaks. Explosive mixtures of gas and air are quickly formed in enclosed places, and they only need a lighted match or a spark to cause disastrous results.

10. Avoid hanging curtains and other draperies near gas jets or other open flames. Remember that the draft from nearby windows may cause fires to spread and make them difficult to extinguish.

11. Use decorative wax candles with caution. Each year some deaths of children and adults are due to placing candles on Christmas trees or using them near flammable materials.

12. Avoid placing articles made of celluloid, pyralin, xylonite, fiberoid, viscoloid, and similar materials, such as combs, toilet articles, etc., upon or near sources of heat, as they are very likely to catch afire. Also remember that articles of these materials should not be worn in the hair as they may readily catch fire and seriously burn the wearer.

13. Permit only experienced persons to install or repair electrical fittings and appliances.

14. Never leave unattended lighted heating or cooking appliances, particularly kitchen ranges and stoves, flatirons, toasters, waffle irons or other equipment of a similar nature.

15. Make sure that when you burn refuse that you do so out-of-doors in a metal container well away from any building. Also be sure that when you leave you have extinguished all smoldering embers.

Fire Extinguishers

Fire-fighting equipment for the ordinary dwelling will usually be limited, by practical considerations, to portable hand apparatus. Principal reliance for extinguishing fires which have gained any appreciable headway must, of course, be placed on outside aid. When a fire occurs, the fire department, if one is available, should always be summoned without delay.

It is, however, true that most household fires start from a small beginning and can in the majority of cases be readily extinguished before they have gained headway and before any considerable damage has been done or risk of personal injury has developed, if the proper means is right at hand and can be promptly applied. The immediate application of a little water or the use of blankets may readily extinguish a small blaze which might later have developed into a disastrous blaze. A partially filled pail of water may often be used effectively. A broom can be used to apply the water in a finely divided state, which is often satisfactory for extinguishing a fire, and also may be used to bring within reach burning draperies or to beat out a small blaze. An ordinary garden hose with nozzle, kept where it can be quickly attached to a water faucet, is also an effective fire-extinguishing device for the area over which its length will permit its application. But water should not be used to combat oil, grease, or electrical fires.

Portable Extinguishers

There are on the market portable hand extinguishers which are specially designed for first-aid fire-fighting, the effectiveness of which has been demonstrated by years of experience. They are much more effective than improvised means, and have the added advantage that,

since they are intended for one purpose only, they can be kept in assigned places where they will be available when needed. It is, therefore, distinctly worthwhile to have one or more good portable fire extinguishers in every household.

In providing first-aid fire-fighting devices for the protection of the household, it is of prime importance that the devices purchased be reliable, and designed and constructed in accordance with recognized standards with regard to safety and performance, such as are defined in Federal specifications or those set up by the Underwriters' Laboratories, or other recognized authorities. Since it is usually not feasible for the householder to make adequate examination and tests, he will have to rely on the results of tests and approval made by others, as evidenced by inspection labels, certifications, or other forms of guaranty.

In the case of Underwriters' Laboratories each extinguisher of a type which has been approved is marked with a distinctive inspection label. This label is usually in the form of a small brass plate attached to the extinguisher near the name plate or forming a part of the name plate itself. This does not mean that all fire-fighting devices which do not bear the Underwriters' Laboratories label are improperly designed and constructed, but that the presence of this label does assure the purchaser that a given extinguisher has been built in accordance with recognized standards.

Portable fire extinguishers are suitable for combating three classes of incipient fires in the home. According to the National Board of

847

Fire Extinguisher Facts			
TYPE	**KINDS OF FIRE**	**HOW TO START**	**DISCHARGE**
Soda Acid	Class A	Turn over	For 2½ gal. size 30'–40' 50–55 sec.
Water Pump	Class A	Pump by hand	
Gas Cartridge	Class A and small Class B	Turn over and pump	
Foam	Class A and Class B	Turn over	
Carbon Dioxide	Class B and Class C and sometimes Class A	Pull pin and open valve	6'–8', about 42 sec. (15-lb. size)
Vaporizing Liquid		Turn handle, pump by hand	20'–30' 45 sec. (1-qt. size)
Dry Chemical		Pull pin and open valve (or press lever), then squeeze nozzle valve	About 14' 22–25 sec. (30-lb. size)

Note: Do not use water-base extinguishers on electrical fires.

Fire Underwriters, those classes of fires are as follows:

(a) Class "A" fires—in ordinary combustible materials (such as wood, paper, textiles, rubbish, etc.) where the quenching and cooling effects of quantities of water or solutions containing large percentages of water is of first importance.

(b) Class "B" fires—in flammable liquids, greases, etc., where a blanketing effect is essential.

There has been a good deal of controversy about the toxic effect of the carbon tetrachloride used in the vaporizing liquid type of hand fire extinguishers. It is recognized that carbon tetrachloride vapor has an anaesthetic effect and if subjected to high temperatures decomposes to some extent, forming toxic gases, including hydrochloric acid and phosgene. The standards of the National Board of Fire Underwriters contain the following caution:

"In using extinguishers of this type, especially in unventilated spaces, such as small rooms, closets, or confined spaces, operators and others should take precautions to avoid the effects which may be caused by breathing the vapors or gases liberated or produced."

Location of Fire Extinguishers

Since no one type of extinguisher is equally effective against all types of fires, it is best to use one which is effective against oil, grease, and electrical fires, and partially effective against rubbish, wood and paper fires. These include carbon dioxide, vaporizing liquid, and dry chemical. However, in a large house, for specific locations, other types should be included.

848

In the basement, add a water pump tank since this is the area where rubbish and papers are usually collected and become a fire hazard. Also keep two buckets of clean sand, one near the furnace and one near the entrance to the basement for use against small spill fires of flammable liquid.

In the kitchen, in an easily available place, have one of the three types recommended for general use. but be sure it is light enough for a woman to handle easily. Here the dangers are rubber, grease and electrical fires.

In a two-story or split-level house, or one that rambles a distance, provide separate extinguishers for the different areas.

In the garage, if there is a water faucet nearby, have a 25-foot length of garden hose ready for im-mediate use. Buckets of sand should also be kept here for use against small spill fires.

Fire Alarms

A small home fire alarm can give the first warning of a fire. Since a large proportion of all fires start in the basement, this would be a good place to install one. Of course, other parts of the house can be similarly protected.

There are three types of alarms: the manual wind-up, battery operated, and electrically operated. The

Vaporizing Liquid (carbon tetrachloride)—to be used against Class B (oil, grease, paint, gasoline) and Class C (electrical) and has some effect on Class A (wood, paper and textiles). This pressurized can is small enough to be kept easily available in even the smallest apartment.

849

Water Pump Tank—to be used against Class A fires (rubbish, paper, and wood, etc.) To prevent freezing and to make sure that the extinguisher will work at temperature as low as 40° below 0, mix anti-freeze into the water.

manual wind-up is least subject to failure. The electrically operated alarm will not work during power failures or electrical failures on the line it is wired on. For one model, its effective area can be extended by simply adding more wire with fire sensitive elements.

What to Do in Case of Fire

Each member of a household should understand how to send in a fire alarm to the fire department. In many cities the fire alarm may be sent in by telephone or from a street fire-alarm box. Some cities require that the alarm be sent in by telephone, and others require that a fire-alarm box be used. Seconds count at the time of a fire, so the proper method should be definitely known, and used.

If sending in a fire alarm by telephone is required or permitted, the telephone number of the fire department should occupy a conspicuous and permanent place at each telephone or telephone extension in the home. In giving information about a fire over the telephone, one should carefully consider what he is doing. What the fire department wants and should know is (a) the number of the house, (b) the name of the street or road, (c) the nearest street corner, and (d) the number of the telephone from which the call is made. A few seconds lost in giving this information are not wasted.

If sending a fire alarm from a fire-alarm box is required or permitted, the location and method of use of the nearest fire-alarm box should be definitely known. Also, if such a method is employed, someone should be stationed in the vi-

cinity of the fire-alarm box or along the route of the responding fire department company to direct it to the fire.

Saving the lives of the occupants of a building on fire should receive first consideration. Many lives have been lost in attempts to put out fires or to save personal belongings.

In case of fire:

1. Collect your thoughts. Keep your mind on what you are doing, Act quickly.

2. Unless you are very sure that you can handle the fire without help, notify the fire department or have someone else do this. Many have been sure until too late.

3. Summon help if anyone is within calling distance.

4. If the blaze is small and you think you can put it out by devices which are available, either

   (a) use a suitable fire extinguisher, or

   (b) use a woolen blanket or rug to smother the fire. Keep the air from the fire, or

   (c) throw water from a garden hose on the fire if such a hose is available. If it is not, throw water from a pail, using a dipper or a broom. Do not use water on an oil or grease fire; use sand or earth from flower pots. Water, especially in small amounts, will cause spattering of burning grease.

   (d) Beat down any draperies, curtains, or light materials causing the blaze, using a wet broom or a long pole. Using the bare hands may result in serious burns.

5. Tie a wet towel or any other material (preferably of wool) over the mouth and nose if you are fight-

ing the fire and are exposed to smoke or flames. More people lose their lives by suffocation than through burning.

6. Place yourself so that you can retreat in the direction of a safe exit without passing through the burning area. Unless you can do something worthwhile, get out of the building.

7. If necessary to go through a room full of smoke, keep close to the floor and crawl on the hands and knees, having covered the mouth and nose with a wet cloth. The drafts and currents cause the smoke to rise and the air nearest the floor is usually the purest.

8. If you have to retreat and all occupants are out of the building or burning portion thereof, cut off the draft by closing doors and windows.

9. Do not jump from a high window unless into a life net. To use a rope or life line, twist the rope or life line around one leg and, holding the feet together, regulate the speed of descent. Otherwise the hands may be painfully injured by friction with the rope or life line, especially if the height is great. Sheets and other articles of bedding will often provide a life line if knots are carefully made so that they will not slip. An extra loop in the knot may avoid this danger. Tie the rope or life line to a bed or other article of furniture which will not pull through the window. The rope or life line should not be thrown out of the window until the instant it is needed. Getting out from an upper story onto a porch or veranda has saved many lives. Such action also affords temporary relief from smoke and heat and also attracts rescuers.

Fireplaces

All fireplaces should be built in accordance with a few simple essentials of correct design if satisfactory performance is to be realized. They should be of a size best suited to the room in which they are to be used from the standpoint of appearance and operation. If too small, they may function properly but do not throw out sufficient heat. If they are too large, a fire that would fill the combustion chamber would be entirely too hot for the room and would waste fuel.

The location of the chimney, which determines the location of

Prefabricated fireplace is easily added in any room of the house and can be installed with a few hand tools. It comes with its own chimney, thereby eliminating expensive masonry work.

Photograph courtesy of Uni-Bilt Division, Vega Industries, Inc.

851

the fireplace, is too often governed by structural considerations only. A fireplace suggests a fireside group and a reasonable degree of seclusion and therefore, especially in the living room, it should not be near doors to passageways of the house.

Characteristics

The principal warming effect of a fireplace is produced by the radiant heat from the fire and from the hot back, sides, and hearth. In the ordinary fireplace practically no heating effect is produced by convection, that is, by air current. Air passes through the fire and up the chimney, carrying with it the heat absorbed from the fire; at the same time outside air of a lower temperature is drawn into the room. The effect of the cold air thus brought into the room is particularly noticeable farthest from the fire.

Modified Fireplaces

The Franklin stove is a type of modified fireplace. There are also modified fireplaces manufactured as units of heavy metal, designed to be set into place and concealed by the usual brickwork or other construction, so that no practical change in mantel design is required by their use. The modifications are built-in standard parts of the fireplace—only the grilles show.

One advantage claimed for modified fireplace units is that the correctly designed and proportioned firebox, manufactured with throat, damper, smoke shelf, and chamber, provides a form for the masonry, thus reducing the risk of failure and assuring a smokeless fireplace. However, there is no excuse for using

incorrect proportions; and the desirability of using a foolproof form, as provided by the modified unit, merely to obtain good proportions should be considered from the standpoint of cost. Even though the unit is well designed, it will not operate properly if the chimney is inadequate; therefore, the rules for correct chimney construction must be adhered to with the modified unit as well as with the ordinary fireplace.

Field tests have proved that, when properly installed, the better designs of modified-fireplace units circulate heat into the cold corners of rooms and will deliver heated air through ducts to adjoining or upper rooms. For example, heat could be diverted to a bathroom from a living-room fireplace.

Sofa and chairs clustered around the fireplace form a conversation area. Fireplace screen contains sparks.

852

Cozy family room in a restored farmhouse boasts brick wall with raised-hearth fireplace and oversized wood mantel.

However, the nature of operation, with the unavoidably large quantity of heated air passing up the stack, makes the inherent over-all efficiency of any fireplace relatively low. Therefore, claims for an increased efficiency of modified fireplaces should be understood merely as constituting an improvement over the ordinary fireplace and not over stoves or central heating plants.

Selecting a Fireplace

When a fireplace is being selected the kind of fuel to be burned should be considered; also, the design should harmonize with the room in proportion and detail.

In general, the wider the opening, the greater should be the depth.

A shallow opening throws out relatively more heat than a deep one of the same width but accommodates smaller pieces of wood; thus it becomes a question of preference between a greater depth which permits the use of large logs that burn longer and a shallower depth which takes smaller-sized wood but throws out more heat.

As a rule, fireplaces on the second floor are smaller than those on the first floor and it is well to follow this practice because the flue height is less for second-floor fireplaces.

Unless a fireplace 6' wide is fully 28" deep, the logs will have to be split, and some advantage of the wide opening will be lost.

A fireplace 30" to 36" wide is generally suitable for a room having 300 square feet of floor. The width should be increased for larger rooms, but all other dimensions should be taken from the table "Recommended Dimensions for Fireplaces."

Units providing for burning gas are often built in to resemble fireplaces.

Pleasing designs result from exercising good taste in use of materials and mantels that suit the room. The essentials for safety and utility, however, should not be sacrificed for style.

In this modified fireplace air enters the inlet, a, from outside and is heated as it rises by natural circulation through the back chamber, c, and the tubes, t, being discharged into the room from the register, b. Air for supporting combustion is drawn into the fire at d and passes between the tubes up the flue. A damper is also provided to close the air inlet.

Construction

The ordinary fireplace is constructed generally with these essentials: (1) that the flue have the proper area, (2) that the throat be correctly constructed and have suitable damper, (3) that the chimney be high enough for a good draft, (4) that the shape of the fireplace be such as to direct a maximum amount of radiated heat into the room, and (5) that a properly constructed smoke chamber be provided.

Dimensions

The table, "Recommended Dimensions for Fireplaces," gives recommended dimensions for fireplaces of various widths and heights.

If a damper is installed, the width of the opening will depend on the width of the damper frame, the size

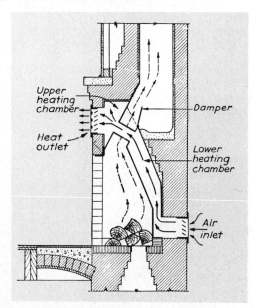

Upper heating chamber

Damper

Heat outlet

Lower heating chamber

Air inlet

Brick hearth makes a perfect table setting for an intimate fireside snack.

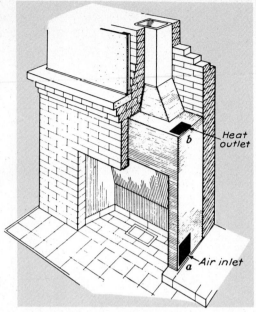

In this fireplace the air is not drawn in directly from outdoors but through the inlet by contact with the metal sides and back of the fireplace, rises by natural circulation, and is discharged back into the room from the outlet, b, or to another room on the same floor or in the second story. The inlets and outlets are connected to registers which may be located at the front of the fireplace. The registers may be located on the ends of the fireplace or on the wall of an adjacent room.

of which is fixed by the width and depth of the fireplace and the slope of the back wall.

The width of the throat proper is determined by the opening of hinged damper cover. The full damper opening should never be less than the flue area. Responsible manufacturers of fireplace equipment give valuable assistance in the selection of a suitable damper for a given fireplace. A well-designed and well-installed damper should be regarded as essential in cold climates.

When no damper is used, the throat opening should be 4 inches for fireplaces not exceeding 4 feet in height.

Prefabricated Fireplace

To fill the need for a low-cost fireplace that eliminates expensive masonry construction, a completely prefabricated fireplace and chimney have been developed. The unit, complete with chimney, can be installed in four to six manhours.

856

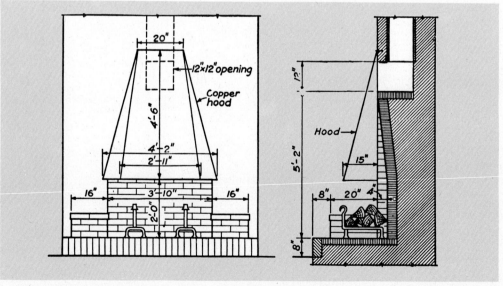

A shallow fireplace, with a copper hood, throws out considerable heat after the hood gets hot. The wall should be of fire resistant masonry.

Free-standing prefabricated fireplace is easily installed by the do-it-yourselfer, is especially favored for vacation homes.

Except for the trim, the complete unit is prime coated and ready to paint with any interior paint to harmonize with the room decorating scheme. A flexible hearth screen comes with the fireplace to prevent sparks from flying out of the fireplace into the room.

Preformed Firebox

Fireplace construction is an exacting art. While some handymen would like to build a fireplace from scratch, others undoubtedly will be content to install a prefabricated fireplace and chimney while others would like to eliminate the complicated firebox construction and do the rest of the work themselves. A preformed metal unit, Heatform, will enable the handyman to eliminate the complicated planning and building of the firebox.

The units are available in different styles so that you can build any type of fireplace—Colonial to Contemporary—around the basic frame. Heatform is a double-walled metal

857

unit consisting of a firebox, throat, dome and heat control damper. It forms a guide around which masonry walls of the fireplace can be built easily and economically.

For those who wish to build a complete unit themselves, there are full details in the remainder of this section.

Hearth

The hearth in conventional fireplaces should be about flush with the floor, for sweepings may then be brushed into the fireplace. When there is a basement, an ash dump located in the hearth near the back of the fireplace is convenient. The dump consists of a metal frame about 5″ by 8″ with a plate, generally pivoted, through which ashes can be dropped into a pit below.

In buildings with wooden floors the hearth in front of the fireplace should be supported by masonry trimmer arches or other fire-resistant construction. Hearths should project at least 16″ from the chimney breast and should be of brick, stone, terra cotta, or reinforced concrete not less than 4″ thick. The length of the hearth should be not less than the width of the fireplace opening plus 16″. Wooden centering under trimmer arches may be removed after the mortar has set, though it is more frequently left in pace.

Wall Thickness

The walls of fireplaces should never be less than 8″ thick, and if of stone they should be at least 12″ thick. When built of stone or hard-burned brick, the back and sides are

858

Recommended Dimensions for Fireplaces							
Opening Width Inches	Height Inches	Depth Inches	Mini-mum back (hori-zontal) Inches	Vertical back wall Inches	Inclined back wall Inches	Outside dimensions of standard rectangular flue lining Inches	Inside diameter of standard round flue lining Inches
24	24	16–18	14	14	16	8½ x 8½	10
28	24	16–18	14	14	16	8½ x 8½	10
24	28	16–18	14	14	20	8½ x 8½	10
30	28	16–18	16	14	20	8½ x 13	10
36	28	16–18	22	14	20	8½ x 13	12
42	28	16–18	28	14	20	8½ x 18	12
36	32	18–20	20	14	24	8½ x 18	12
42	32	18–20	26	14	24	13 x 13	12
48	32	18–20	32	14	24	13 x 13	15
42	36	18–20	26	14	28	13 x 13	15
48	36	18–20	32	14	28	13 x 18	15
54	36	18–20	38	14	28	13 x 18	15
60	36	18–20	44	14	28	13 x 18	15
42	40	20–22	24	17	29	13 x 13	15
48	40	20–22	30	17	29	13 x 18	15
54	40	20–22	36	17	29	13 x 18	15
60	40	20–22	42	17	29	18 x 18	18
66	40	20–22	48	17	29	18 x 18	18
72	40	22–28	51	17	29	18 x 18	18

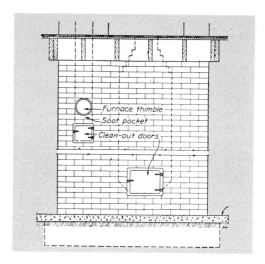
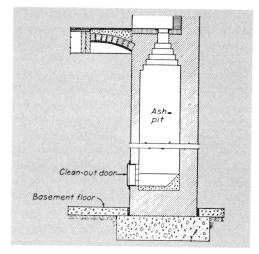

The ashpit should be of tight masonry and should be provided with a tightly fitting iron clean-out door and frame about 10″ by 12″. A clean-out for the furnace flue as shown is sometimes provided.

often not lined with firebrick, but it is better to use firebrick laid in fire clay. When firebricks are laid flat with the long edges exposed there is less danger of their falling out. They are generally placed on edge, however, forming a 2″ protection, in which case metal ties should be built into the main brickwork to hold the 2″ firebrick veneer in place. Thick metal backs and sides are sometimes used as lining. When a grate for burning coal or coke is built in, fire-brick at least 2″ thick should be added to the fireplace back unless the grate has a solid iron back and is only set in with an air space be-hind it.

Jambs

The jambs should be wide enough to give stability and a pleasing ap-pearance; they are frequently faced with ornamental brick or tile. For an opening 3″ wide or less, a 12″ or 16″ width is generally sufficient, depending on whether a wood mantel is used or the jambs are of exposed

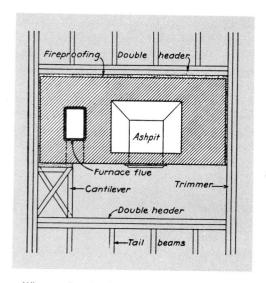

Where a header is more than 4′ in length, it should be doubled, as shown. Headers supporting more than four tail beams should have ends supported in metal joist hangers. The framing may be placed ½″ from the chimney because the masonry is 8″ thick.

859

masonry. The edges of a wood mantel should be kept at least 8″ from the fireplace opening. For wider openings and large rooms, similar proportions should be kept.

Lintel

Lintels of ½″x3″ bars, 3½″x 3½″x¼″ angle irons, or damper frames are used to support the masonry over the opening or ordinary fireplaces. Heavier lintel irons are required for wider openings.

Where a masonry arch is used over the opening, the jambs should be heavy enough to resist the thrust of the arch. Arches over openings less than 4′ wide seldom sag, but sagging is not uncommon in wider fireplaces, especially where massive masonry is used.

Throat

The sides of the fireplace should be vertical up to the throat, or damper opening. The throat should be 6″ to 8″ or more above the bottom of the lintel and have an area not less than that of the flue and a length equal to the width of the fireplace opening. Starting 5″ above the throat, the sides should be drawn in to equal the flue area.

Proper throat construction is necessary to a successful fireplace and the builder must make certain that the side walls are carried up perpendicularly until the throat is passed and that the full length of opening is provided.

Smoke Shelf and Chamber

The smoke shelf is made by setting the brickwork back at the top of the throat to the line of the flue wall for the full length of the throat. Its depth may vary from 6″ to 12″ or more, depending on the depth of the fireplace.

The smoke chamber is the space extending from the top of the throat up to the bottom of the flue proper and between the side walls. The walls should be drawn inward 30° to the vertical after the top of the throat is passed and smoothly plastered with

Cast-iron insert reduces the size of this bedroom fireplace opening; door shuts it off completely when not in use.

White brick fireplace and hearth stand out dramatically against mustard gold of the shag carpet and deep-toned walls.

cement mortar not less than ½″ thick.

Damper

A properly designed damper affords a means of regulating the draft and prevents excessive loss of heat from the room when the fire is out. A damper consists of a cast-iron frame with a lid hinged so that the width of the throat opening may be varied from a closed to a wide-open position. Various patterns are on the market, some designed to support the masonry over the opening, others requiring lintel irons.

A roaring pine fire may require a full-throat opening, but slow-burning

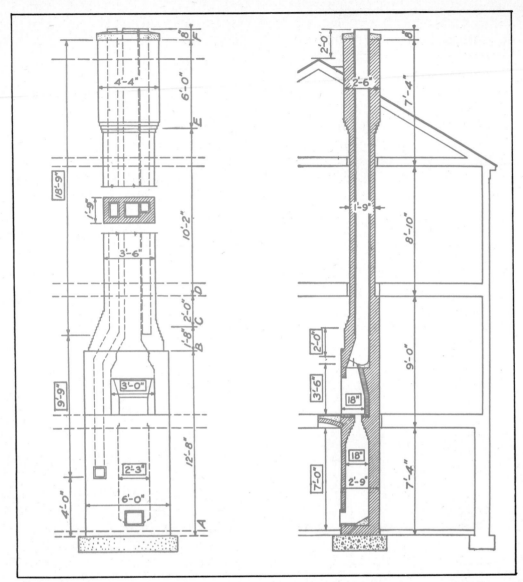

Diagram showing front view and cross section of an entire chimney such as is commonly built to serve a furnace, fireplace, and kitchen stove. Two sets of dimensions are given; those in rectangles refer to the approximate sizes of the voids or openings, the others refer to the outside dimensions of the brickwork. These are used in estimating the quantities of brick required.

862

hardwood logs may need only 1" or 2" of opening. Regulating the opening according to the kind of fire prevents waste of heat up the chimney. Closing the damper in summer keeps flies, mosquitos, and other insects from entering the house down the chimney.

Flue

The area of lined flues should be a twelfth or more of the fireplace opening, provided the chimney is at least 22' in height, measured from the hearth. If the flue is shorter than 22' or if it is unlined, its area should be made a tenth or more of the fireplace opening. A fireplace which, for instance, has an opening of 7.5 square feet, or approximately 1,080 square inches, needs a flue area of approximately 90 square inches; a rectangular flue, 8½"x18", outside dimensions, or a round flue with a 12" inside diameter might be used, as these are the nearest commercial sizes of lining. It is seldom possible to obtain lining having exactly the required area, but the inside area should never be less than that prescribed above. A 13"x13" flue was selected for convenience when combining with the other flues. If the flue is built of brick and is unlined, its area should be approximately one-tenth of the fireplace opening, or 108 square inches. It would probably be made 8"x16" (128 square inches) because brickwork can be

laid to better advantage when the dimensions of the flue are multiples of 4".

The Table, "Sizes of Fireplace Flue Linings," is convenient in selecting the proper size of flue or for determining the size of fireplace opening for an existing flue. The area of the fireplace opening in square inches is obtained by multiplying the width by the height, both measured in inches.

Refer to *CHIMNEY CON-STRUCTION.*

Smoky Fireplace

When a fireplace smokes, it should be examined to make certain that the essential requirements of construction have been fulfilled. If the chimney is not stopped up with fallen brick and the mortar joints are not loose, note whether nearby trees or tall structures cause eddies down the flue. To determine whether the fireplace opening is in correct proportion to the flue area, hold a piece of sheet metal across the top face of the fireplace opening and then gradually lower it, making the opening smaller until smoke does not come into the room. Mark at the lower edge of the metal on the sides of the fireplace. The opening may then be reduced by building in a metal shield or hood across the top so that its lower edge is at the marks made during the test. The trouble can generally be remedied in another way by increasing the height of the flue.

Cleaning Brickwork

When the brickwork around the fireplace becomes soiled, it may be scrubbed with a brush dipped into a solution of 1 tablespoonful of tri-

Sizes of Fireplace Flue Linings[1]		
Area of fireplace opening	Outside dimensions of standard rectangular flue lining	Inside diameter of standard round flue lining
Square inches	Inches	Inches
	8½ x 8½	10
600	8½ x 13	10
800	8½ x 18	12
1,000	8½ x 18	12
1,200	13 x 13	12
1,400	13 x 13	15
1,600	13 x 18	15
1,800	13 x 18	15
2,000	13 x 18	15
2,200	18 x 18	18
2,400	18 x 18	18
2,600	18 x 18	18
2,800	18 x 18	18
3,000		

[1]Based on a flue area equal to one-twelfth the fireplace opening.

863

Heavy timber mantel is set into the brick of this huge cooking fireplace in a 170-year-old home.

sodium phosphate to a gallon of water. Rinse off with clear water, and then dry with a cloth.

But if the bricks are stained, they may need to be bleached. For this purpose use about 1¼ lbs. of oxalic acid crystals in a gallon of warm water, adding sufficient lime or whiting to form a soft paste. (Caution: oxalic acid is a poison, and it must be handled carefully!) Use a broad knife or spatula to spread this paste over the stained parts of the brickwork. Let it remain about 15 minutes, then scrape off the paste. Wash the bricks with clear water, then dry with a cloth.

Should the cleaning or bleaching not remove the dirt or stains from the bricks, try putting a thin oil stain over them, choosing the same or perhaps a little darker color than the bricks. This will give them a uniform dark appearance.

Hearth Tiles

To keep the hearth looking its best, wash the tiles with warm, soapy water, then rinse with clear water. When completely dry, rub a coat of wax over them. This not only adds to their good appearance but makes the tiles more dirt-resistant.